MEDICAL FINANCIAL LITERACY

The Healthcare Provider Reference Guide for Financial Education

ANDRE HAME

Copyright © Andre Hame 2024

All rights reserved. No part of this publication may be reproduced, distributed, or transmitted in any form or by any means, including photocopying, recording, or other electronic or mechanical methods, without the prior written permission of the publisher, except in the case of brief quotations embodied in critical reviews and certain other noncommercial uses permitted by copyright law.

Contents

Chapter 1: Financial Literacy Fundamentals 1

Chapter 2: Budgeting and Debt Management 10

Chapter 3: Credit Scores 19

Chapter 4: Investing 25

Chapter 5: Stock Market 32

Chapter 6: Real Estate 39

Chapter 7: Alternative Investments 46

Chapter 8: Retirement Planning 53

Chapter 9: Tax Strategies 59

Chapter 10: Insurance 67

Chapter 11: Risk Management 73

Chapter 12: Practice Financial Management 79

Chapter 13. Business Ownership 85

Chapter 14: Estate Planning 91

Chapter 15: Major Life Events 96

Chapter 16: Career Transitions 102

Chapter 17: Financial Education 107

Chapter 18: Financial Plans 112

Found an error?

Typo?

Dot out of place?

Suggestion for content or illustration?

We welcome any tips, suggestions, or corrections for this guide. Please e-mail brownvase123@gmail.com. We will do best to accommodate all appropriate suggestions into the next edition.

Please use this simple format for emails:
- o   Your Name
- o   Your E-Mail
- o   Your Phone Number
- o   Your Comment/Illustration suggestion
- o   Reference or Support for your Comment (optional)

Chapter 1

Financial Literacy Fundamentals

> *"Financial literacy is not an end in itself, but a means to an end: a tool that can help individuals achieve their personal and financial goals."*
>
> **Annamaria Lusardi**

Financial literacy serves as the cornerstone for long-term financial success. Understanding diverse financial ideas and concepts enables people to make informed and successful decisions regarding their financial resources. Physicians, who frequently encounter unique financial obstacles and possibilities, must learn financial literacy in order to achieve long-term financial security and independence.

Financial goals are defined, quantifiable objectives that you want to achieve with your cash. Setting specific short-term, medium-term, and long-term financial goals helps you create concrete plans and provides direction for your financial decisions. To begin, physicians should specify their goals, such as saving for a down payment on a home, repaying college loans, or establishing a retirement fund. To stay on track, divide these goals into smaller, more doable activities and establish deadlines for each.

Net worth is the entire value of your assets minus your obligations. Calculating your net worth on an annual basis allows you to keep track of your financial situation and make necessary changes to enhance it. Physicians should identify all assets, including savings, investments, and real estate, and deduct all obligations, including college loans, mortgages, and credit card debt. Use this data to establish a baseline and set targets for increasing net worth over time.

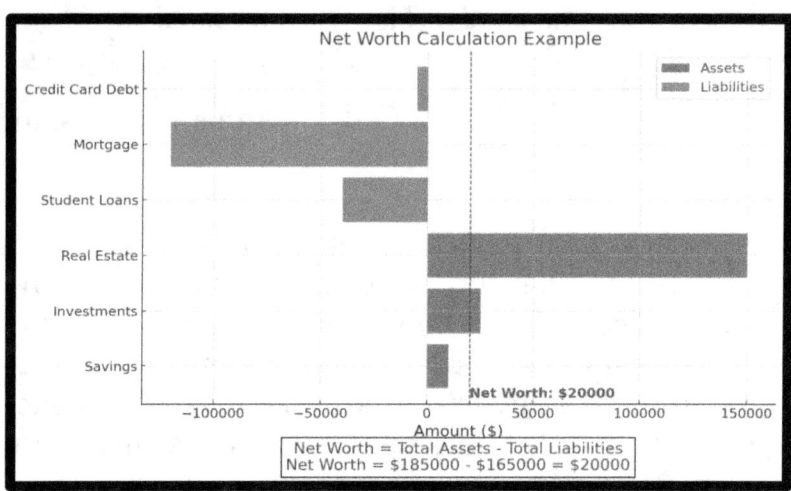

Cash flow is the movement of money into and out of your bank accounts. Monitoring your monthly cash flow guarantees that your income covers your expenses and allows you to identify areas where you may save money. Physicians can prepare a complete cash flow statement by detailing all sources of income and costs. Review this statement on a regular basis to guarantee positive cash flow and make necessary adjustments to spending patterns.

The opportunity cost refers to the possible benefits you miss out on when you choose one option over another. Considering opportunity costs in all financial decisions allows you to make better informed and advantageous judgments. For example, when selecting whether to invest in additional schooling or a new business venture, consider the prospective returns and benefits of each option versus what you may forego.

Inflation is the rate at which the overall level of prices for goods and services grows, reducing buying power. Including inflation in your long-term financial planning guarantees that your savings and investments stay up with the rising cost of living. Physicians should utilize inflation-adjusted estimates when preparing for retirement or establishing long-term financial objectives to ensure they can retain their preferred lifestyle in the future.

Compound interest is the process of generating interest on both the initial principal and any previous interest earned. Investing in accounts that pay compound interest greatly increases the growth of your money over time. Physicians can benefit from compound interest by investing in retirement accounts like 401(k)s or IRAs and reinvesting dividends to optimize profits.

Liquidity is the ease with which an asset can be converted to cash without influencing its market price. Maintaining a portion of your assets in liquid form is critical for satisfying short-term demands and crises. Physicians should save a portion of their money in highly liquid accounts, such as a high-yield savings account or money market fund, to cover unforeseen needs.

Asset allocation is a method for balancing risk and reward by spreading investments among several asset categories, such as stocks, bonds, and real estate. Regularly monitoring and modifying your asset portfolio helps you align your risk tolerance with your financial objectives. Physicians should diversify their investment portfolios to reduce risk and maximize rewards. Regularly rebalance the portfolio to maintain the appropriate asset allocation.

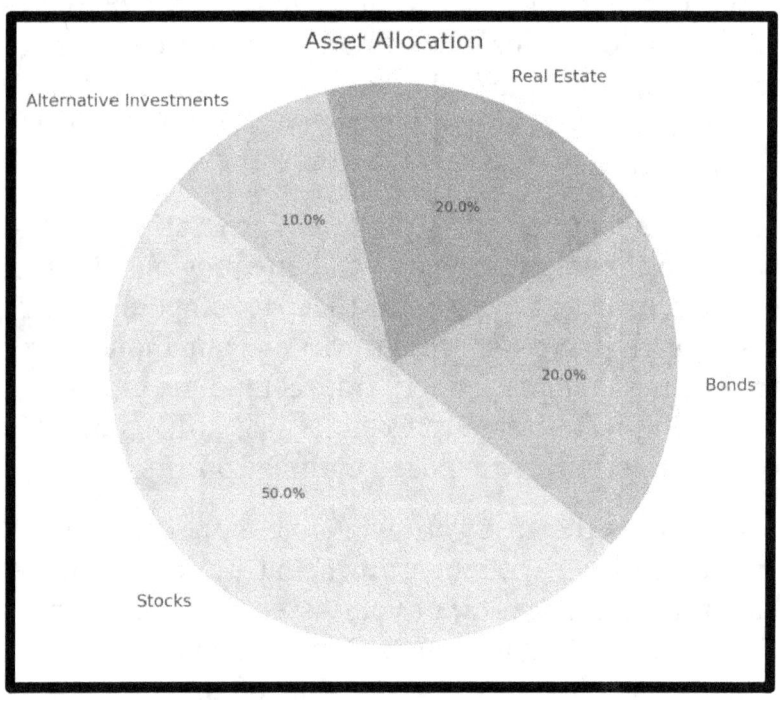

Diversification entails spreading investments across multiple assets to lessen risk. Diversifying your investment portfolio protects you from severe losses in any one investment. Physicians can diversify by investing in a variety of equities, bonds, real estate, and alternative assets. Use mutual funds or ETFs to get broad diversification with little effort.

An emergency fund is a savings account set up for unexpected needs such as medical emergencies, car repairs, or job loss. Building and maintaining an emergency fund that covers three to six months of living expenses is critical for financial stability. Physicians should prioritize emergency funds over other investments. Set up automatic payments to a designated savings account to ensure that the fund grows consistently.

The savings rate is the percentage of income set aside for saving and investing. Saving at least 20% of your salary will help you get closer to financial freedom and achieve your financial goals. Physicians should assess their monthly budget to seek ways to boost their savings rate. Consider automating contributions to retirement and other savings accounts.

Financial independence is defined as having enough personal money to survive without actively working for fundamental needs. Developing a plan for financial independence gives you greater flexibility in your job and life choices. Physicians should determine their financial independence number, which is the amount of funds required to pay living expenses without relying on employment income. Create a savings and investment strategy to achieve this goal over time.

The expense ratio is the percentage of an investment's assets allocated to administrative and other operating expenses. Choosing investments with low expense ratios maximizes your long-term gains. When making financial decisions, physicians should examine the expense ratios of mutual funds and exchange-traded funds. To keep your investment expenditures to a minimum, choose low-cost index funds.

Risk tolerance refers to an individual's willingness and ability to withstand market volatility and probable losses. Assessing your risk tolerance and investing properly ensures that your investment strategy is consistent with your comfort level and financial objectives. Physicians can use online risk tolerance surveys to assess their risk level. Adjust your asset portfolio based on your risk tolerance and financial objectives.

SMART goals entails developing financial objectives that are specific, measurable, attainable, relevant, and time-bound. Using the SMART criteria for all financial goals adds clarity and concentration, making it easier to track and achieve them. Physicians should set their financial goals and organize them into manageable measures. To stay on target, review progress on a regular basis and make adjustments as appropriate.

SMART goals
Specific
Measurable
Achievable
Relevant
Time-bound

Short-term goals are objectives that must be met within a year, such as repaying a small debt or saving for a vacation. Setting attainable short-term goals generates momentum and immediate wins. Physicians should emphasize short-term goals that have a major influence on their financial health, such as saving for an emergency or paying off high-interest debt.

Medium-term objectives are those set for one to five years, such as saving for a down payment on a house or financing a large purchase. Planning and saving for medium-term goals takes greater discipline and commitment. Physicians should devise a savings strategy for each medium-term goal, devoting a percentage of their income to designated savings accounts or investment vehicles.

Long-term goals are ambitions that last more than five years, such as saving for retirement or supporting a child's education. Investing in long-term savings accounts enables these objectives to profit from compound interest. Physicians should save for long-term goals through retirement accounts like a 401(k) or IRA, as well as education savings plans like a 529 plan. To stay on track, assess donations on a regular basis and change them accordingly.

Monitoring progress means frequently assessing and adjusting financial strategies to ensure that you stay on track to meet your objectives. Using budgeting tools and financial planning software allows you to monitor your progress and make the required modifications. Physicians should plan regular financial check-ups to measure progress toward their objectives. Make changes to the budget, savings, and investment plans as needed.

High-interest debt refers to debt with high interest rates, such as credit card debt, which can swiftly undermine financial stability. Prioritizing high-interest debt repayment frees up funds for savings and investing. Physicians should develop a debt repayment strategy that focuses on paying off high-interest debt first. Consider employing debt snowball or debt avalanche tactics to speed payback.

Living beyond your means entails spending more than you make, resulting in financial stress and debt accumulation. Sticking to a realistic budget will help you maintain your financial health and prevent debt. Physicians should keep track of all income and costs to verify that spending is within their budget. Identify places where spending might be decreased and redirect money toward financial objectives.

The lack of an emergency fund exposes you to unforeseen expenses, causing you to incur debt or liquidate investments. Setting up an emergency fund is an important first step in financial planning. Physicians should emphasize saving for an emergency fund, with the goal of covering three to six months' living expenses. Use high-yield savings accounts to earn interest on your emergency fund.

Inadequate insurance can expose you to financial losses due to health difficulties, accidents, or lawsuits. Regularly evaluating and updating your insurance policy assures proper coverage. Physicians should check their insurance coverage every year, including health, disability, life, and malpractice insurance. Adjust the coverage as needed to guarantee complete protection.

Neglecting retirement savings might lead to a large reduction in retirement funds. Saving for retirement early and taking advantage of employer-sponsored plans can help you build a solid retirement fund. Physicians should make regular contributions to their retirement accounts, taking advantage of company matching and tax-advantaged accounts. To optimize your retirement savings, gradually increase your contributions.

Actionable Steps

☐ Set specific, measurable short-term, medium-term, and long-term financial goals.

☐ Calculate and track net worth annually.

☐ Build and maintain an emergency fund covering 3-6 months of living expenses.

☐ Diversify investments across various asset classes.

☐ Prioritize paying off high-interest debt.

Chapter 2

Budgeting and Debt Management

> *"A budget is telling your money where to go instead of wondering where it went."*
>
> Dave Ramsey

Budgeting is the foundation of financial planning, which involves developing a strategy for spending and saving money. Effective budgeting is critical for physicians due to high levels of student debt, changing salaries, and the expenditures associated with starting and running a business. Choose a budgeting technique that best fits your lifestyle, such as zero-based budgeting or the envelope system.

Fixed expenses are consistent, unchangeable costs such as rent or mortgage payments. Listing all of your fixed expenses allows you to better understand your basic financial commitments and ensure that money is allocated effectively. Monitor these expenses to determine how they affect your entire budget.

Variable expenses, such as utilities and groceries, fluctuate from month to month. Tracking these expenses helps you find spending trends and places where you may cut prices to save more money. Use budgeting tools to keep track of your variable spending.

Discretionary spending includes non-essential expenses like dining out and leisure. Limiting discretionary expenditures is critical to freeing up funds for savings and debt repayment. Set a monthly limit on discretionary spending and stick to it.

Cash flow management involves tracking income and expenses in order to maintain a positive cash flow. Regularly assessing your cash flow ensures that your income meets all costs and savings goals, thereby reducing financial stress. Create a complete cash flow statement and update it on a monthly basis.

An emergency fund is a savings account for unexpected needs, such as medical bills or car repairs. Building and maintaining an emergency fund that covers three to six months of living expenses is critical for financial stability. Set up automatic transfers to a designated savings account to continually grow this investment.

Short-term savings entails laying aside funds for future expenses within a year. Using savings or money market accounts for these goals allows you to plan for immediate financial requirements without depleting your long-term resources. Identify short-term objectives and allocate funding accordingly.

Long-term savings are used for purposes that last more than five years, such as retirement or education. Investing in long-term savings accounts allows the funds to increase over time, meeting your future financial demands. For long-term savings, use retirement accounts such as 401(k)s or IRAs.

Automation entails setting up automatic transfers to savings accounts. Automating savings contributions assures continuous progress toward your financial goals without requiring manual intervention. Create automated transfers for both short- and long-term savings.

Expense reduction is the practice of discovering and reducing unnecessary expenses. Regularly evaluating your budget allows you to identify areas for cost savings and debt reduction. Conduct a monthly expense assessment and discover areas where you may cut back.

Debt might take the form of student loans, credit card debt, mortgages, or auto loans. Listing your debts allows you to better grasp their terms and prioritize repayment plans. Make a precise inventory of your debts, including interest rates and monthly payments.

Interest rates are the cost of borrowing money, represented as a percentage. Focusing on paying off high-interest debt first reduces interest expenses and speeds up repayment. Compare the interest rates on all debts and prioritize the ones with the highest rates.

The principal is the original amount borrowed on a loan. Tracking the principal amounts of your debts allows you to monitor repayment progress and keep motivated to pay off your loans. Regularly monitor your loan statements to keep track of principal decreases.

Secured vs. unsecured debt contrasts loans with collateral (secured) with those without collateral (unsecured). Understanding the difference allows you to prioritize which debts to pay off first based on risk and interest rates. Determine if your obligations are secured or unsecured before devising a repayment strategy.

Good vs. bad debt distinguishes debt utilized for future investments (good) from debt used to depreciate assets (bad). Concentrate on minimizing bad debt while managing good debt wisely. Make a plan to repay bad debt and manage good debt.

The debt snowball strategy entails paying off the smaller obligations initially to gain momentum. This strategy is useful for staying motivated by gaining small victories in debt repayment. List your debts from smallest to greatest, then begin paying off the smallest first.

The debt avalanche strategy focuses on paying off the loans with the highest interest rates first to reduce interest costs. This strategy results in the greatest long-term savings on interest payments. Sort your loans by interest rate and prioritize the ones with the highest rates.

Debt consolidation involves combining various loans into a single loan with a lower interest rate. Consider consolidation if it lowers your overall interest rate and makes payments easier. Investigate consolidation possibilities and decide whether they are beneficial to your position.

Refinancing involves replacing a current loan with a new one at a reduced interest rate. Consider refinancing options to lower monthly payments and interest charges, especially for significant debts such as mortgages or school loans. Compare refinancing options and apply if they result in savings.

A balance transfer is the process of shifting high-interest debt to a credit card with a lower interest rate. Balance transfers can help you save money on interest, but be aware of transfer fees and be sure to pay off the balance before the introductory rate ends. Before transferring, research balance transfer deals and ensure that you understand the terms.

Federal and private loans have varied periods, interest rates, and repayment alternatives. Understanding your loan types allows you to choose the optimal repayment approach and capitalize on potential rewards. Check your loan documentation to see if it is federal or private.

Income-driven repayment plans tailor payments to your income and family size. If you have federal student loans and want to make modest payments, look into income-driven options. Contact your loan servicer to discuss income-driven repayment options.

Loan forgiveness programs allow remaining loan balances to be forgiven after making qualifying payments for a set period of time. Consider possibilities such as Public Service Loan Forgiveness (PSLF) for possible relief. Check the qualifying requirements and apply if you qualify.

Deferment and forbearance allow for the temporary suspension or lowering of loan payments owing to financial difficulties. Use these solutions only when absolutely required, and consider the long-term impact on your debt. Contact your loan servicer to request a postponement or forbearance if necessary.

Regular budget evaluations include monthly or quarterly assessments of your revenue and expenses. Schedule regular assessments to monitor progress, spot trends, and make any required adjustments to stay on target. Set a reminder to evaluate and alter your budget as needed.

Budgeting apps, spreadsheets, and financial documents all serve as tracking tools. Use apps such as Mint or YNAB to effectively monitor your budget and ensure accurate financial planning. Select a tracking tool that works for you and use it consistently.

Adjusting for life changes entails making changes to your budget to account for large income or cost fluctuations. To ensure that your budget remains relevant, revisit it after big life events such as a job shift, marriage, or childbirth. If your financial status has changed significantly, update your budget to reflect this.

Overspending means spending more than your budget permits, which causes financial hardship. To keep your finances in order, stick to your budget and prevent impulse purchases. Monitor your spending habits and make changes to stay within your budget.

Underestimating expenses means not including all probable costs in your budget. Include a cushion for unexpected expenses to minimize financial surprises and keep your budget accurate. Regularly evaluate your budget and make adjustments for any unexpected spending.

Not saving enough means not prioritizing savings in your budget. Make saving a non-negotiable portion of your budget in order to develop financial security and attain your objectives. Every month, set aside a portion of your paycheck for savings, and increase your contributions as your income grows.

Ignoring debt means failing to factor debt payments into your budget. Set aside money each month for debt repayment to lower your financial load and enhance your financial health. Make debt repayment a priority in your budget and create a plan to pay it off.

Lack of flexibility occurs when your budget is not adjusted to reflect changes in your financial situation. Be adaptable and change your budget as needed to stay on target and handle changing situations. Regularly review your budget and adapt it to reflect changes in income or expenses.

Budgeting applications are tools for generating and managing budgets. Use programs like Mint or YNAB to make budgeting easier and help you stay within your budgetary boundaries. Examine various budgeting apps and select one that meets your demands.

Financial planning software includes programs for complete financial planning. Consider using software such as Quicken or Personal Capital to manage your finances and plan for the future. Investigate financial planning software options and choose one that fits your needs.

Debt management tools are resources for managing and repaying debt. Use debt calculators and credit counseling organizations to create a debt payback plan that is right for you. Investigate debt management techniques and seek expert help if necessary.

Budgeting and debt management are critical skills for attaining financial stability and independence. Physicians can gain control of their finances, minimize financial stress, and work toward long-term financial goals by learning and adopting good budgeting practices and debt repayment plans. Regularly reviewing and changing your budget helps you stay on track and respond to changes in your financial circumstances.

Actionable Steps

☐ Choose a budgeting technique that fits your lifestyle (e.g., zero-based budgeting, envelope system, etc.).

☐ Track all fixed, variable, and discretionary expenses to understand spending patterns and identify areas for cost savings.

☐ Build and maintain an emergency fund covering 3-6 months of living expenses with automatic transfers to a designated savings account.

☐ Regularly create and update a comprehensive cash flow statement to ensure income covers all expenses and savings goals.

☐ Use budgeting tools (apps, spreadsheets, financial software) consistently to monitor and adjust your budget as needed.

Chapter 3

Credit Scores

"Your credit score is a direct reflection of your financial habits and decisions."

Jean Chatzky

Credit scores are numerical estimates of a person's creditworthiness based on their credit history. These scores are critical for obtaining loans, attaining low interest rates, and even renting apartments or landing specific jobs. Maintaining a decent credit score can help physicians finance their school, buy a home, and start a business. Regularly monitoring and controlling your credit score is critical for financial stability.

The FICO score is the most extensively used credit scoring methodology, with a range of 300 to 850. Understanding your FICO score and the factors that influence it allows you to take action to enhance or maintain a decent score. Regularly verify your FICO score with your credit card company or a credit monitoring service. Aim for a score above 700 to gain access to the greatest financial products and interest rates.

VantageScore is an alternative credit score formula that ranges from 300 to 850. Knowing both your FICO and VantageScore provides a complete picture of your credit health. Compare your VantageScore to your FICO score to detect any disparities and learn how different factors can affect each score.

Credit usage is the percentage of your current credit card balance compared to your credit limit. Keeping your credit use around 30% is excellent for maintaining a decent credit score. Pay off debt before the statement's closing date to lower reported use. Request credit limit increases to improve your utilization ratio without incurring additional debt.

Payment history is a record of your timely and late payments. It is the most important aspect of your credit score. Set up automatic payments to ensure you never miss a deadline. If you miss a payment, make it as quickly as possible and contact your creditor to see if the late payment can be removed from your credit report.

The length of your credit history refers to the term of your credit accounts. Keeping older accounts open and in good standing will help enhance your credit score. Avoid closing old credit cards, even if you don't use them frequently. If you need to terminate an account, prioritize newer ones to keep your credit history intact.

The term "new credit" refers to the quantity of recently opened credit accounts and hard inquiries. Opening multiple new accounts in a short period of time may potentially reduce your credit score. Apply for new credit only if you absolutely need it. When shopping for loan rates, do so quickly (e.g., within 30 days) to reduce the impact of several inquiries.

Credit mix refers to the diversity of credit accounts, including credit cards, mortgages, and vehicle loans. Having a varied range of credit types can improve your score. If you just have one sort of credit, try adding another, such as a small personal loan or a secured credit card, to diversify your credit portfolio.

Making timely payments is critical for maintaining a decent credit score. To ensure you never miss a due date, set up automated payments for all of your credit cards. To stay on top of approaching due dates, set payment reminders and calendar alerts. If you find it difficult to handle many payments, try debt consolidation to make your payment plan easier.

Reducing credit utilization is critical for maintaining a healthy credit score. Reduce credit card balances to maintain your utilization below 30%. Make many payments throughout the month to keep the balance low. If you have significant amounts, pay them off first before making any new purchases with your credit cards.

Correcting inaccuracies on credit reports helps to maintain an accurate credit score. Equifax, Experian, and TransUnion offer free annual credit reports through AnnualCreditReport.com. Check your reports for errors, such as inaccurate balances or accounts that do not belong to you. File disputes with credit bureaus to correct inaccuracies and guarantee that your reports contain accurate information.

Avoiding new credit inquiries reduces the potential negative influence on your score. Limit new credit applications to necessary necessities like a mortgage or auto loan. When shopping for a loan, do so quickly to reduce the impact of several inquiries. Soft inquiries allow you to check your credit score without harming it.

Building credit entails developing and maintaining healthy credit habits. If you have no credit history or are rebuilding it, try getting a secured credit card or becoming an authorized user on someone else's credit card. Make little purchases and pay off the entire sum each month to demonstrate prudent credit utilization.

Credit reports contain complete information about your credit account and history. AnnualCreditReport.com offers free annual credit reports from each of the three main bureaus. Check the reports for accuracy and completeness. Look for typos, unusual accounts, and indications of identity fraud.

Reading credit reports allows you to better understand your credit history and find opportunities for improvement. Check your personal information to make sure it is accurate. Check account information, including balances and payment history, for accuracy. Take note of any public documents, such as bankruptcies or liens, and understand how they can affect your credit score.

To dispute problems on your credit report, contact the credit bureaus and correct any inconsistencies. Find mistakes, such as inaccurate account balances or unknown accounts. File a dispute online, over the phone, or by mail, along with supporting proof. Follow up to confirm that corrections are completed and reflected in your report.

Your credit score influences loan acceptance and interest rates. Higher scores make it easier to obtain loans and pay lower interest rates. If you have a low credit score, work to improve it before applying for big loans. Compare loan offers to obtain the most favorable terms and rates.

Your credit score might have an impact on both renting and employment. Landlords frequently utilize credit scores to judge rental applications. Some businesses examine credit ratings as part of the employment process, especially for professions that require financial responsibility. Maintaining a decent credit score will increase your chances of finding housing and jobs.

Your credit score can influence your insurance premiums. Many insurers utilize credit-based insurance ratings to set vehicle and homeowner's insurance prices. A higher credit score might lead to reduced insurance premiums. Check your credit report for accuracy and make efforts to enhance your score to save money on insurance.

Consistently checking your credit score allows you to be informed about your credit health. Check your credit ratings and reports from various sources on a regular basis. Use credit monitoring services to obtain notifications about big changes. Take immediate action if you find any irregularities or symptoms of identity theft.

Responsible credit utilization is essential for having a decent credit score. Borrow only what you can repay, and avoid taking on more debt than you can handle. Keep previous accounts open to protect the duration of your credit history. Use credit responsibly by making on-time payments and keeping balances low.

Long-term practices like financial discipline and avoiding excessive debt help to build a solid credit score. Always pay your bills on time and keep your credit card balance low. Make prudent credit decisions and prioritize keeping a good credit profile.

Credit monitoring programs such as Experian, TransUnion, Equifax, Credit Karma, and Credit Sesame allow you to track your credit score and report. Use these applications to stay up-to-date on changes to your credit profile and receive notifications for critical modifications. Choose an app that meets your needs and use it frequently.

Actionable Steps

☐ Regularly monitor your credit score and obtain your credit reports from online

☐ Maintain credit utilization below 30% by managing credit card balances and requesting credit limit increases.

☐ Make timely payments by setting up automatic payments and reminders for all credit accounts.

☐ Correct inaccuracies on credit reports by filing disputes with credit bureaus to ensure accurate information.

☐ Diversify your credit mix by having a variety of credit types, such as credit cards, mortgages, and personal loans.

Chapter 4

Investing

"Investing should be more like watching paint dry or watching grass grow. If you want excitement, take $800 and go to Las Vegas."

Paul Samuelson

Investing is an essential part of accumulating wealth and accomplishing financial objectives. Understanding the fundamentals of investing allows physicians to make more educated decisions that are consistent with their risk tolerance and financial goals. Begin by understanding the fundamental investment principles and tactics.

Risk vs. reward refers to the balance between the potential return on investment and the risk of loss. Higher potential gains are typically associated with greater risk. Assess your risk tolerance to find the best balance for your investing portfolio. Use online risk tolerance surveys to assess your level of comfort with risk. When analyzing your risk tolerance as a physician, keep career security and income potential in mind.

Diversification entails spreading assets across multiple asset classes in order to lessen risk. A diverse portfolio reduces the impact of poor performance on any one investment. To build a well-balanced portfolio, physicians should diversify their investments among stocks, bonds, real estate, and alternative assets. Review your portfolio on a regular basis to ensure that it remains diverse, and make adjustments as needed based on your financial goals and market conditions.

Asset classifications include equities, bonds, real estate, and cash. Each asset type has unique risk and return characteristics. Understanding these distinctions enables you to allocate investments based on your financial objectives and risk tolerance. For example, equities often generate bigger returns but are more volatile, whereas bonds provide more predictable income with reduced risk. To balance risk and reward, allocate a part of your portfolio to each asset class.

Stocks indicate ownership in a firm and have the possibility for capital growth and dividends. They are ideal for long-term growth but have a higher level of volatility. To diversify risk, invest in a diverse portfolio of individual stocks, stock mutual funds, and exchange-traded funds. Consider sectors with a lower correlation to the healthcare business to diversify your portfolio.

Bonds are debt securities that pay interest and refund principal at maturity. They provide more stability and lower risk than equities. Include a combination of government, municipal, and corporate bonds in your portfolio to generate a consistent income stream while reducing total volatility.

Mutual funds and exchange-traded funds (ETFs) aggregate money from multiple participants to buy a diverse portfolio of equities or bonds. They provide diversification and competent management at a reduced cost. Choose low-cost index funds or ETFs to save fees while ensuring broad market exposure. To maximize your earnings, seek out funds with a proven track record and reasonable expense ratios.

The investment horizon is the amount of time you plan to hold an investment before needing the funds. Longer investing horizons generally allow for more risk-taking because there is more time to recover from market changes. Align your investments with your investment time horizon to maximize profits and manage risk. For example, if you are preparing for retirement in 20 years, you may be able to be more active with your stock investments.

Investment accounts consist of taxable brokerage accounts, retirement accounts (401(k), IRA), and tax-advantaged accounts (HSA). Each account type has unique tax implications and benefits. To optimize your savings, select the appropriate accounts for your investing goals and make use of tax-advantaged accounts. Contribute to your 401(k) or IRA on a regular basis, and if qualified, consider a Health Savings Account (HSA), which provides triple tax advantages.

Dollar-cost averaging is an investment technique in which you invest a consistent amount regardless of market conditions. This strategy mitigates the effects of market volatility and decreases the average cost per share over time. Set up automatic contributions to your investing accounts so that you can continuously invest a percentage of your income. This technique promotes consistent wealth accumulation and reduces the desire to time the market.

Rebalancing is the process of occasionally modifying your portfolio to preserve your intended asset allocation. Over time, certain investments may outperform others, altering your allocation. Regular rebalancing ensures that your portfolio remains in line with your risk tolerance and investing objectives. Schedule rebalancing every year or semi-annually, and modify your investments to fit your target allocation.

Buy and hold is a long-term investment strategy in which you purchase securities and keep them for an extended period of time, regardless of market swings. This method reduces transaction costs while capitalizing on the market's long-term upward trend. Avoid frequent trading and instead focus on high-quality investments that you believe will outperform over time.

Value and growth investing are two distinct investment approaches. Value investing seeks out discounted equities with excellent fundamentals, whereas growth investing looks for companies with great growth potential. Diversify your portfolio by including both value and growth stocks to capitalize on changing market conditions. Research and choose investments depending on your financial objectives and risk tolerance.

There are two techniques for investing: passive and active. Passive investment entails tracking a market index with low-cost index funds, or ETFs, whereas active investing involves selecting individual securities that outperform the market. Physicians may prefer passive investing because it is less expensive and requires less time commitment. Some people may choose active investing if they have the knowledge and time to actively manage their accounts.

Compound interest is the process of generating interest on both the initial principal and any previous interest earned. Investing in accounts that pay compound interest greatly increases the growth of your money over time. Select investing accounts and products that enable your earnings to compound, such as dividend reinvestment plans (DRIPs) and growth-oriented mutual funds.

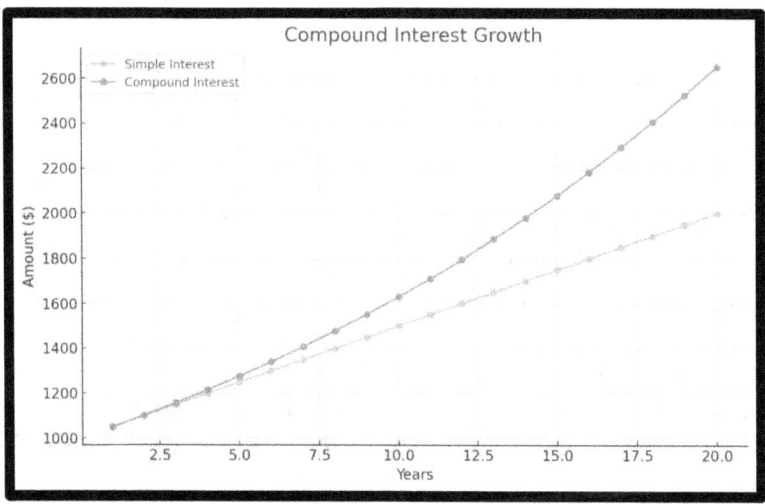

Tax concerns are a crucial part of investing. Different investments and accounts have different tax implications. Understand the tax status of your investments in order to maximize your after-tax earnings. Use tax-advantaged accounts, such as IRAs and 401(k), to postpone or avoid paying taxes on investment gains. Consider tax-efficient investing techniques, such as keeping investments for more than a year, to benefit from long-term capital gains tax rates.

Investment costs might reduce your returns over time. Be aware of any fees linked to your investments, such as management fees, expense ratios, and trading commissions. To minimize expenses and increase returns, consider low-cost investment options such as index funds and ETFs. Review your costs on a regular basis and, if possible, look for lower-cost options.

Professional counsel might be beneficial to physicians who lack the time or expertise to handle their investments. Consider working with a financial counselor who understands the specific financial requirements of physicians. Look for a fee-only advisor who serves as a fiduciary, which means they must operate in your best interests. Schedule regular assessments with your advisor to verify your investing strategy is in line with your financial objectives.

Investing is an essential part of accumulating wealth and establishing financial stability. Understanding these investment fundamentals and taking concrete steps can help physicians build a diversified and balanced portfolio that matches their financial goals and risk tolerance. Regularly assess and change your investments to stay on track and maximize your long-term profits.

Actionable Steps

☐ Assess your risk tolerance and diversify investments across multiple asset classes.

☐ Regularly contribute to appropriate investment accounts (401(k), IRA, HSA) for tax benefits.

☐ Implement dollar-cost averaging by setting up automatic contributions.

☐ Rebalance your portfolio annually or semi-annually to maintain asset allocation.

☐ Minimize investment costs by choosing low-cost index funds and ETFs.

Chapter 5

Stock Market

"The stock market is designed to transfer money from the Active to the Patient."

Warren Buffett

Stock market investing has a high potential for long-term gain. Understanding how the stock market works and creating a solid investment strategy can help physicians accumulate money. Begin by studying the fundamental concepts and practical procedures for investing in stocks.

Stocks indicate ownership in a firm and have the possibility for capital appreciation and dividends. Investing in a diverse portfolio of individual stocks, mutual funds, and ETFs spreads risk. Before investing, do your research and look for firms with excellent fundamentals and growth potential. Diversify your stock investments across industries and sectors to mitigate risk.

Stock exchanges, such as the New York Stock Exchange (NYSE) and NASDAQ, are platforms for buying and selling equities. Understanding how these exchanges work allows you to navigate the stock market. Access these markets and trade stocks using trustworthy online brokerage accounts. Make sure the brokerage has a user-friendly platform and cheap trading fees.

Market capitalization is the total market value of a company's outstanding shares. Market capitalization determines whether a company is considered large-cap, mid-cap, or small-cap. Diversify your portfolio by including stocks from various market capitalization groups to balance risk and return. Large-cap stocks are more stable, whereas small-cap companies have stronger growth potential but greater volatility.

Blue-chip stocks are shares of large, well-established, financially stable corporations with a track record of consistent profitability. These stocks are generally regarded as safe investments with consistent dividends. Add blue-chip stocks to your portfolio for stability and income. Research and choose blue-chip firms with a proven track record and strong financials.

Growth stocks are shares of firms that are predicted to grow faster than the market as a whole. These stocks typically reinvest earnings to stimulate growth rather than pay dividends. Set aside a portion of your portfolio for growth stocks to maximize potential rewards. Concentrate on companies in innovative industries with great development potential.

Dividend stocks pay out monthly dividends to shareholders, ensuring a consistent revenue source. These stocks are usually from established corporations with consistent earnings. Consider dividend stocks to boost your income and improve the stability of your portfolio. Reinvest dividends to capitalize on compound growth over time.

Stock market indices such as the Dow Jones Industrial Average (DJIA), S&P 500, and NASDAQ Composite monitor the performance of a group of stocks. Understanding these indices allows you to measure market trends and benchmark your portfolio's performance. Consider investing in index funds or ETFs that mirror these indices to gain broad market exposure and diversity.

Fundamental analysis entails assessing a company's financial health and performance in order to estimate its intrinsic worth. Earnings per share (EPS), the price-to-earnings ratio (P/E), and return on equity (ROE) are all important indicators. Use fundamental research to find undervalued stocks that have a high potential for growth. Review financial data and analyze company performance to make sound investment decisions.

Technical analysis employs previous price and volume data to forecast future stock price movements. Moving averages, RSIs, and candlestick charts are all common tools. While technical analysis can help with fundamental analysis, it should not be the main basis for investment decisions. Use technical analysis to determine entry and exit points for stock transactions.

Dividend reinvestment plans (DRIPs) allow investors to automatically reinvest dividends to buy more stock. Participating in DRIPs allows your investment to grow through compounding. Set up DRIPs for your dividend-paying equities to increase long-term gains with minimal effort.

Dollar-cost averaging is an investment technique that involves investing a set amount of money at regular intervals, regardless of market conditions. This strategy mitigates the effects of market volatility and decreases the average cost per share over time. Set up automatic contributions to your investing accounts so that you can continuously invest a percentage of your income.

Buy and hold is a long-term investment strategy in which you purchase securities and keep them for an extended period of time, regardless of market swings. This method reduces transaction costs while capitalizing on the market's long-term upward trend. To save money and taxes, focus on high-quality assets rather than frequent trading.

Value investing is purchasing inexpensive stocks that are predicted to appreciate in value over time. Look for firms that have good fundamentals but are currently undervalued in the market. Research and choose value-added companies based on financial statistics and performance metrics.

Growth investing focuses on companies with strong growth potential. These stocks often do not pay dividends since earnings are reinvested to promote future growth. Allocate a percentage of your portfolio to growth stocks for higher potential profits, especially in creative and fast expanding industries.

Index funds are mutual funds or ETFs that track the performance of a specific market index, such as the S&P 500. They provide extensive market exposure with cheap fees. Consider index funds as a diversified, low-cost investment choice. They offer an easy approach to investing in a broad market segment while earning market-average returns.

ETFs (Exchange-Traded Funds) are investment funds that trade on stock markets, comparable to stocks. They provide diversification by tracking multiple indices, sectors, or asset classes. Use ETFs to obtain exposure to particular market segments or investment concepts. They are versatile and can be bought and sold throughout the trading day.

Mutual funds pool the money of multiple investors to invest in a diverse portfolio of stocks, bonds, and other securities. They provide diversification as well as professional management, and they are managed by professional fund managers. To optimize gains, invest in mutual funds with a great track record and low expense ratios.

Rebalancing is the process of occasionally modifying your portfolio to preserve your intended asset allocation. Over time, certain investments may outperform others, altering your allocation. Regular rebalancing ensures that your portfolio remains in line with your risk tolerance and investing objectives. Schedule rebalancing every year or semi-annually, and modify your investments to fit your target allocation.

Tax concerns are a crucial part of investing. Different investments and accounts have different tax implications. Understand the tax status of your investments in order to maximize your after-tax earnings. Use tax-advantaged accounts, such as IRAs and 401(k), to postpone or avoid paying taxes on investment gains. Consider tax-efficient investing techniques, such as keeping investments for more than a year, to benefit from long-term capital gains tax rates.

Investment costs might reduce your returns over time. Be aware of any fees linked to your investments, such as management fees, expense ratios, and trading commissions. To minimize expenses and increase returns, consider low-cost investment options such as index funds and ETFs. Review your costs on a regular basis and, if possible, look for lower-cost options.

Professional counsel might be beneficial to physicians who lack the time or expertise to handle their investments. Consider working with a financial counselor who understands the specific financial requirements of physicians. Look for a fee-only advisor who serves as a fiduciary, which means they must operate in your best interests. Schedule regular assessments with your advisor to verify your investing strategy is in line with your financial objectives.

Actionable Steps

- ☐ Diversify your stock investments across various industries and sectors.
- ☐ Use a reliable online brokerage account with low trading fees.
- ☐ Balance your portfolio with large-cap, mid-cap, and small-cap stocks.
- ☐ Include blue-chip and dividend stocks for stability and income.
- ☐ Perform fundamental analysis to assess company value and growth potential.

Chapter 6

Real Estate

"Real estate cannot be lost or stolen, nor can it be carried away. Purchased with common sense, paid for in full, and managed with reasonable care, it is about the safest investment in the world."

Franklin D. Roosevelt

Real estate investment provides chances for both income generation and capital appreciation. Understanding the many forms of real estate investments and how to handle them can help physicians diversify their portfolios and accumulate wealth. Begin by studying the foundations and practical methods of investing in real estate.

Real estate investments include residential and commercial properties, as well as real estate investment trusts (REITs). Residential assets, including single-family homes and multi-family apartments, can generate rental revenue while increasing in value. Commercial properties, such as office buildings and retail spaces, have larger earning potential but are more complex. REITs allow you to invest in real estate without directly owning the property, providing liquidity and diversification.

Residential properties can provide rental revenue and increase in value. Buying rental properties entails looking for acceptable locations, calculating possible rental income, and managing tenants. Investigate local real estate markets to find high-demand regions with future growth possibilities. Calculate the prospective rental income and expenses to ensure profitability. If you don't want to handle renters yourself, hire property management companies.

Commercial properties have a higher earning potential but are more complex. These include office buildings, retail establishments, and industrial properties. Investing in commercial real estate necessitates an awareness of market demand, tenant requirements, and lease agreements. Analyze market trends and economic factors to find profitable commercial assets. Consider teaming up with seasoned commercial real estate investors or hiring professional management.

Real estate investment trusts (REITs) enable investors to purchase stock in a firm that owns and manages income-generating real estate. REITs provide liquidity and diversification while eliminating the need for direct property management. Invest in publicly traded REITs to acquire exposure to the real estate market at a lower cost. Examine REITs with solid track histories and diverse property assets.

Property management entails managing rental properties, which includes tenant screening, rent collection, and maintenance. Effective property management ensures consistent rental income and property value appreciation. If you do not want to handle properties directly, employ a professional property management company. To keep tenants and protect your investment, inspect buildings on a regular basis and respond quickly to maintenance issues.

Understanding mortgage alternatives and interest rates is required when financing a real estate transaction. Shop around for the best mortgage rates and terms to fund your real estate projects. Consider fixed-rate mortgages for consistent payments or adjustable-rate mortgages for lower beginning rates. Evaluate how mortgage terms affect your cash flow and investment returns.

Down payments are an important part of financing real estate. A higher down payment lowers the loan amount and monthly payments. A 20% down payment is recommended to avoid private mortgage insurance (PMI) and achieve better loan terms. Save for a down payment by setting aside a portion of your monthly income and reducing unnecessary costs.

The loan-to-value (LTV) ratio is the ratio of the loan to the value of the property purchased. A lower LTV ratio decreases lender risk and may result in more favorable loan terms. To qualify for advantageous mortgage rates, keep your LTV ratio below 80%. Calculate your LTV ratio before applying for a mortgage to better understand your borrowing ability.

Interest rates influence the cost of borrowing and the overall profitability of real estate projects. Monitor current interest rates and economic developments to determine the optimum moment to finance a property.

Lock in a low interest rate while conditions are favorable to lower long-term borrowing costs.

Home equity is the difference between a property's market value and its outstanding mortgage balance. Building home equity boosts your net worth and gives you leverage for future investments. Pay down your mortgage and consider making home upgrades to increase property value and equity.

Appreciation refers to the increase in property value over time. Investing in places with strong appreciation potential can result in big capital gains. Look at local market trends, economic development, and infrastructure developments to find high-growth areas. To maximize appreciation benefits, hold properties for an extended period of time.

Depreciation is the decline in property value caused by wear and tear, which can be mitigated by regular maintenance and improvements. To reduce depreciation, schedule frequent property inspections and handle any maintenance concerns as they arise. Consider making improvements and upgrades to increase property value and attract high-quality tenants.

Leverage is the use of borrowed funds to fund real estate ventures, which increases the potential for returns. Leverage can boost returns, but it also introduces risk. Use leverage wisely by keeping a healthy loan-to-value ratio and ensuring rental revenue meets mortgage payments and costs. To protect yourself from market downturns, avoid excessive leverage.

Cash flow management is critical for sustaining profitable real estate ventures. Ensure that rental income exceeds mortgage payments, property taxes, insurance, and maintenance expenses. Create a cash flow statement for each property to keep track of income and expenses. Set up funds for unanticipated maintenance and vacancies to ensure good cash flow.

Lease agreements are contracts between landlords and renters that specify rental terms and conditions. Create clear and thorough leasing agreements to safeguard your interests and avoid problems. Include information about the rent amount, payment due dates, security deposits, maintenance obligations, and lease duration. Lease agreements should be reviewed and updated on a regular basis to ensure that they meet legal requirements.

Tenant screening is critical for finding dependable tenants who pay their rent on time and maintain the property. Perform a full background check, including credit history, employment verification, and rental references. Set up a regular screening process to ensure fair and effective tenant selection. Use expert tenant screening services to simplify the process and prevent risk.

Property owners must maintain and repair their properties on a continuous basis. Regular maintenance preserves property value and ensures tenant satisfaction. To avoid costly repairs, schedule routine inspections and handle maintenance issues as soon as they arise. Budget for upkeep and create a list of dependable contractors for emergency repairs.

Real estate tax factors include property taxes, mortgage interest deductions, and depreciation. Understanding the tax consequences of real estate might help you maximize your returns. Consult a tax professional to maximize deductions and comply with tax laws. Keep comprehensive records of all property-related expenses to ensure proper tax filing.

The 1031 exchange allows investors to defer capital gains taxes by reinvesting the profits from the sale of an investment property in a comparable property. This method helps to increase wealth by delaying tax bills. Consult a tax professional to learn about the rules and benefits of a 1031 exchange. Plan your investments to capitalize on this tax-deferral opportunity.

Real estate market analysis entails examining market circumstances, trends, and economic indicators in order to make sound investment decisions. Consider issues like supply and demand, vacancy rates, rental yields, and local economic growth. Use market analysis tools and reports to find profitable investment opportunities. Stay educated about market developments so that you may alter your investment strategy properly.

Professional counsel can be quite helpful when navigating the difficulties of real estate investing. Consider hiring a real estate agent, property manager, or financial advisor specializing in real estate. Seek expert help with property acquisition, management, and finance. Regularly assess your real estate portfolio with your advisors to ensure it is in line with your financial objectives.

Research and education are essential for successful real estate investing. Continue to educate yourself on real estate market trends, investment ideas, and property management practices. Use credible sources of information, such as real estate investment books, online courses, and trade periodicals. Stay informed on legal and regulatory changes affecting real estate so that you may adjust your investing plan as needed.

Actionable Steps

☐ Diversify investments across residential properties, commercial properties, and REITs.

☐ Shop for the best mortgage rates and terms.

☐ Hire professional property management if needed.

☐ Ensure rental income exceeds expenses.

☐ Regularly analyze market trends and legal requirements.

Chapter 7

Alternative Investments

"Successful investing is about managing risk, not avoiding it."

Benjamin Graham

Alternative investments allow you to diversify your portfolio beyond typical equities and bonds. Understanding the many forms of alternative investments and their distinct characteristics can help physicians improve returns and reduce risk. Begin by understanding the basics and practical procedures for investing in alternative assets.

Private equity is an investment in private enterprises that are not publicly traded. These investments can provide large returns, but they also carry more risk and have less liquidity. Investigate private equity firms and funds to find prospective investment opportunities. Before investing in a company, consider its track record, investment plan, and management team. Diversify your private equity assets to mitigate risk.

Venture capital focuses on supporting early-stage businesses with great growth potential. These investments can result in big rewards if the company succeeds, but they also represent a high risk. Analyze the business concept, market potential, and management team of a startup to assess venture capital options. Diversify your venture capital assets to spread risk among several firms. Keep track of your money and be prepared for unexpected losses.

Hedge funds are pooled investment funds that use a variety of tactics to achieve high returns. These methods may include long-short equities, arbitrage, or derivatives trading. Hedge funds are often only available to accredited investors due to their high risk. Investigate hedge fund managers and strategies to locate those that match your investing objectives and risk tolerance. Before investing, carefully consider hedge fund performance and fee structures.

Commodities are physical assets such as gold, silver, oil, and agricultural products. Investing in commodities can help you hedge against inflation while also diversifying your portfolio. You can buy commodities directly or invest in commodity-focused ETFs and mutual funds. Monitor commodity market trends and economic factors to help you make investment decisions. Consider the costs of storage and insurance for tangible goods.

Precious metals, including gold and silver, are popular investments for mitigating economic uncertainty and inflation. You can buy real metals, futures contracts, or precious metal ETFs. Store physical metals securely, taking into account storage and insurance expenses. Monitor market movements and geopolitical developments that could affect precious metal prices. Diversify your investment in precious metals to reduce risk.

Cryptocurrency is a digital or virtual currency that employs encryption for security. Bitcoin, Ethereum, and other cryptocurrencies have significant growth potential but are extremely volatile. Invest in cryptocurrency via trusted exchanges and wallets. Diversify your bitcoin holdings and keep up with legislative developments and market trends. Be aware of the security dangers involved with digital currencies and take precautions to protect your investment.

Rare collectibles include art, antiques, and wine. These investments can grow in value, but they need specialist understanding and involve liquidity risk. Investigate the market for your preferred collection and get guidance from specialists. To preserve the value of collectibles, they should be properly stored and insured. Attend auctions and network with other collectors to remain current on market trends.

Crowdfunding enables investors to aggregate cash online to support a variety of initiatives and enterprises. Platforms such as Kickstarter and Indiegogo allow you to invest in companies, real estate, and other ventures. Examine crowdfunding options by considering the project's business model, market potential, and management team. Understand the risks involved, as many programs fail to produce the promised results. Diversify your investments across several crowdfunding initiatives to reduce risk.

Peer-to-peer lending refers to lending money directly to individuals or businesses using online platforms. These loans can provide better returns than regular savings accounts, but they also carry more risk. Conduct thorough research on peer-to-peer lending platforms and borrower profiles. Diversify your loans among several borrowers to lessen the chance of default. Monitor the performance of your loans and reinvest repayments for compound returns.

Angel Investment provides cash to early-stage businesses in exchange for stock ownership. This sort of investment has the potential for high rewards, but it also carries significant risk. Analyze the startup's business concept, market potential, and management team before making an investment decision. Participate in angel investor networks to gain access to deal flow and conduct due diligence alongside other investors. Diversify your angel investments to mitigate risk.

Art is an alternative investment that can grow dramatically over time. Investing in art demands a great sense of value and understanding of market trends. Consult with art consultants and visit galleries and auctions to expand your expertise. Maintain the condition and value of your art collection by properly storing and insuring it. Diversify your art investments by collecting works from a variety of artists, genres, and periods.

Wine as an investment entails purchasing and holding good wines that increase in value over time. Identify investment-grade wines by researching reputed wine merchants and auction houses. To protect the quality and value of wine, keep it in appropriate storage conditions. Track market trends and the performance of your wine assets. Consider broadening your wine portfolio by selecting wines from various areas and vintages.

Timberland investing entails buying and maintaining forested land for timber production. This investment can generate consistent earnings from wood sales and land appreciation. Look at timberland investment prospects and consider partnering with experienced forestry managers. Keep track of the market conditions for timber and land prices. Diversify your forestry investments by purchasing properties in many locations.

Farmland investing entails purchasing agricultural land for crop production or renting it to farmers. This investment has the ability to generate consistent revenue and increase the value of the land. Look into agricultural investment alternatives and consider partnering with expert farm managers. Keep track of market circumstances for crops and land prices. Diversify your agricultural investments by purchasing properties in various regions and types of agriculture.

The purchase of a patent, trademark, or copyright rights is an example of intellectual property investment. These investments may generate revenue through licensing fees or royalties. Investigate intellectual property opportunities and assess their potential for commercialization. Collaborate with intellectual property attorneys to handle legal challenges. Diversify your intellectual property investments to mitigate risk.

When investing in alternative assets, it is vital to exercise due diligence. Before committing to an investment, conduct thorough research and evaluation. Evaluate the risks, possible returns, and market circumstances. Consult with professionals and consultants to acquire valuable insights and avoid errors. Maintain a diverse portfolio to reduce risk.

Risk management entails recognizing and addressing any risks in your alternative investment portfolio. Create a risk management approach that incorporates diversification, due diligence, and ongoing monitoring. Set limitations on the amount of funds used for high-risk investments. To control risk, monitor your assets on a frequent basis and alter your portfolio accordingly.

Liquidity is an important aspect of alternative investments. Many alternative assets are less liquid than traditional investments, making it difficult to sell them promptly and at a reasonable price. Consider each investment's liquidity and make sure your portfolio contains enough liquid assets. Plan for the long term and be willing to keep illiquid investments until they reach their full potential.

Professional assistance might be useful when negotiating the complexities of alternative investments. Consider engaging with financial planners, investment consultants, or alternative asset experts. Seek advice on investing decisions, risk management, and portfolio diversification. Regularly assess your alternative investment portfolio with your advisors to ensure it is in line with your financial objectives.

Research and education are critical for effective alternative investments. Continue to educate yourself on various forms of alternative investments, market trends, and investment strategies. Use credible sources of information, such as investment books, online courses, and trade periodicals. Stay informed on legal and regulatory changes affecting alternative investments so that you may adjust your approach as needed.

Actionable Steps

☐ Diversify your investments across private equity, venture capital, hedge funds, and REITs.

☐ Invest in commodities and precious metals to hedge against inflation.

☐ Use trusted exchanges and wallets for cryptocurrency investments.

☐ Participate in peer-to-peer lending and crowdfunding for additional income sources.

☐ Seek professional advice and stay informed on market trends and legal changes.

Chapter 8

Retirement Planning

"The question isn't at what age I want to retire, it's at what income."

George Foreman

Retirement planning is an essential component of financial stability and independence. Understanding the various retirement accounts and techniques available can aid physicians in developing a solid retirement plan. Begin by studying the foundations and practical strategies for successful retirement planning.

Retirement Planning Timeline

- **20s**: Start saving early, open a retirement account
- **30s**: Increase savings rate, diversify investments
- **40s**: Maximize contributions, review investment strategy
- **50s**: Catch-up contributions, focus on asset allocation
- **60s**: Review withdrawal strategies, consider Social Security benefits

There are various types of retirement savings accounts, such as 401(k), IRA, Roth IRA, SEP IRA, and SIMPLE IRA, each with its own tax advantages and contribution restrictions. Regular contributions to these accounts can help you maximize your retirement savings. Take advantage of employer-sponsored plans, especially those that provide matching contributions.

A 401(k) is an employer-sponsored retirement plan in which employees can contribute pre-tax income. Contributions are tax-deferred until withdrawn. If your employer offers a match, contribute enough to receive the entire match. To balance risk and profit, diversify your 401(k) investment portfolio. Automate contributions to maintain constant savings and alter them as needed to boost your savings rate.

Individuals can contribute pre-tax income to an IRA, and the investments grow tax-deferred until they are withdrawn. If you do not have access to an employer-sponsored plan or want to enhance your retirement savings, consider opening an IRA. A standard IRA provides immediate tax benefits, while a Roth IRA allows for tax-free withdrawals in retirement. Diversify your IRA investments across asset types to maximize growth while managing risk.

Roth IRAs are funded using after-tax income, providing for tax-free growth and withdrawals throughout retirement. Contribute to a Roth IRA if you anticipate being in a higher tax bracket in retirement. Use a Roth IRA to diversify your tax risk throughout retirement. To handle the tax implications, consider gradually converting regular IRA holdings to Roth IRAs.

SEP IRAs (Simplified Employee Pensions) are intended for self-employed people and small business owners.

Contributions are tax deductible and increase tax deferred. If you earn money from your own business and want to maximize your retirement savings, consider a SEP IRA. Contribute up to 25% of your net earnings to a SEP IRA and invest in a variety of assets to build a balanced and diverse portfolio.

The SIMPLE IRA (Savings Incentive Match Plan for Employees) is a retirement plan designed for small businesses and self-employed individuals. Employees and employers both have the opportunity to contribute. If you own a small business, you should consider a simple IRA since it is easier to administer and costs less. Match employee donations to encourage participation. Set up automatic contributions to maintain constant savings.

Catch-up contributions allow those over the age of 50 to contribute more to their retirement plans. Use catch-up contributions to increase your retirement savings as you approach retirement age. Increase your 401(k) and IRA contributions if you are eligible. Plan to boost your savings as part of your retirement strategy.

Retirement income requirements should be calculated to ensure that you save enough to maintain your preferred lifestyle. Calculate your estimated retirement expenses, such as housing, healthcare, and leisure activities. Retirement calculators can help you estimate how much you'll need to save to reach your retirement goals. Base your savings rate and investing plan on your forecasts.

Social Security benefits provide a source of income throughout retirement. Understand how your benefits are calculated and when the optimum time is to begin collecting them. Delaying Social Security benefits may raise your monthly payouts. Create a Social Security strategy that will supplement your other retirement income sources. Consider spousal and survivor benefits as part of your strategy.

Required Minimum Distributions (RMDs) are mandated distributions from retirement accounts beginning at age 72. Prepare for RMDs by learning the rules and estimating the amounts. Avoid penalties by withdrawing the required amount each year. RMDs should be incorporated into your entire retirement income strategy to minimize tax repercussions.

Retirement income strategies include diversifying income streams from several sources. Combine Social Security, retirement account withdrawals, pensions, and other investments to generate a consistent income. Use a withdrawal strategy that strikes a balance between income and capital preservation. Consider the 4% rule as a guideline for making consistent withdrawals.

Annuities can provide a steady income in retirement. If you require a consistent income source, consider including annuities in your retirement plan. Examine various types of annuities, including fixed, variable, and immediate annuities, to choose the best fit for your needs. Be mindful of the costs and terms related to annuities.

Health Savings Accounts (HSAs) provide three tax benefits: tax-deductible contributions, tax-free growth, and tax-free withdrawals for eligible medical costs. If your health plan has a high deductible, consider contributing to an HSA. Use HSA money to offset healthcare expenses in retirement. Keep receipts for medical expenses so you can refund yourself tax-free later.

Long-term care insurance can help safeguard your retirement funds from the high costs of long-term care. If you are concerned about your future care needs, look into long-term care insurance and consider acquiring one. Compare policy details, pricing, and coverage alternatives. Plan for the possibility of requiring long-term care as part of your retirement strategy.

Estate planning is an integral part of retirement preparation. Make a complete estate plan that includes a will, trusts, and powers of attorney. Designate beneficiaries for your retirement savings and keep them updated on a regular basis. Consider the tax consequences of transferring assets to heirs. Consult with an estate planning professional to ensure that your estate plan satisfies your objectives and legal requirements.

Investment diversification is critical for risk management and maximizing returns in your retirement portfolio. Diversify your investments among asset classes, including equities, bonds, and real estate. To keep the asset allocation you like, rebalance your portfolio on a regular basis. As you approach retirement, adjust your investment strategy to lower risk and protect capital.

Tax-efficient investing entails ways to reduce taxes on your retirement resources. Use tax-advantaged accounts, such as Roth IRAs and HSAs, to decrease your tax bill. Consider the tax implications of various investing strategies and account withdrawals. Plan your withdrawals intelligently to help you manage your tax bracket in retirement.

Professional counsel can be crucial when it comes to retirement planning. Consider hiring a financial planner who specializes in retirement. Seek advice on investing, tax, and exit options. Regularly examine your retirement plan with your advisor to ensure it is in line with your objectives and needs.

Research and instruction are critical for effective retirement planning. Continue to educate yourself on retirement planning ideas, investment possibilities, and tax legislation. Use credible sources of knowledge, such as retirement planning books, online courses, and financial journals. Stay updated on changes in Social Security, tax laws, and healthcare so that you may alter your strategy properly.

Actionable Steps

☐ Contribute regularly to retirement accounts (401(k), IRA, Roth IRA, SEP IRA, SIMPLE IRA) to maximize savings.

☐ Diversify investments across asset classes (stocks, bonds, real estate) and rebalance regularly.

☐ Calculate retirement income requirements and adjust savings rate accordingly.

☐ Plan for Required Minimum Distributions (RMDs) starting at age 72.

☐ Consider professional financial advice to optimize retirement strategies and stay informed on changes in tax laws and Social Security.

Chapter 9

Tax Strategies

"In this world, nothing can be said to be certain, except death and taxes."

Benjamin Franklin

Tax techniques are vital for increasing your wealth while decreasing your tax liability. Understanding various tax-saving strategies can allow physicians to keep more of their hard-earned money. Start by studying the principles and practical strategies for efficient tax planning.

The marginal tax rate is the rate at which your final dollar of income is taxed. Knowing your marginal tax rate helps you comprehend the implications of earning more money. Plan your income and deductions to maximize your tax bracket. Use tax-efficient assets to reduce your total tax burden. Consider municipal bonds, which are frequently exempt from federal and state taxes.

The effective tax rate is the average rate at which your entire income is taxed. To calculate your effective tax rate, divide your entire tax liability by your total income. Use this information to determine your overall tax efficiency. Implement tactics to reduce your effective tax rate, such as increasing deductions and credits. Regularly assess your tax situation to seek areas for improvement.

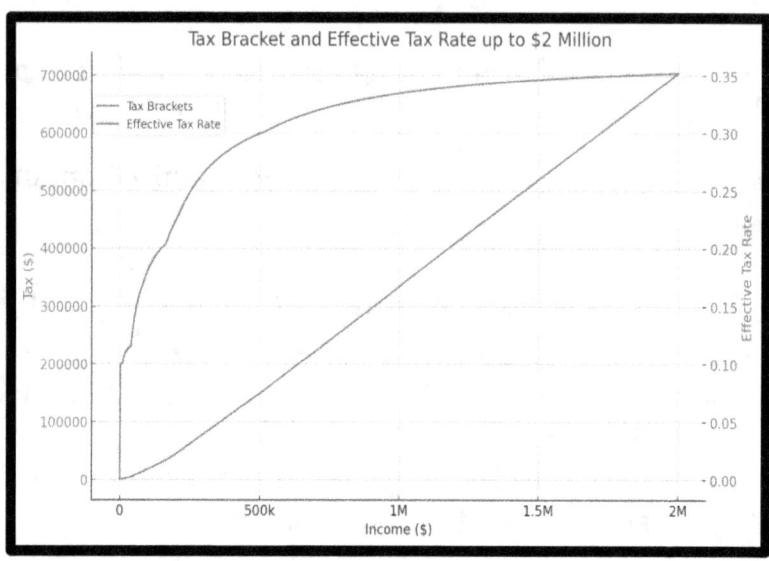

Tax brackets are income ranges that are taxed at different rates. Understanding your tax bracket allows you to manage your income and deductions more effectively. Structure your income to avoid being forced to pay a higher tax rate. Consider delaying income or increasing deductions to help manage your tax bracket. For example, if a bonus would move you into a higher tax rate this year, you might delay it until the following year.

The standard deduction is a predetermined cash amount that lowers your taxable income. Claim the standard deduction if it exceeds your itemized deductions. Understand the standard deduction amount for your filing status and budget your deductions accordingly. Keep track of allowable spending to assess whether itemizing is more helpful. To verify that you are taking full advantage of your deductions, use tax software or talk with a tax professional.

Itemized deductions allow you to deduct certain expenses from your taxable income. Mortgage interest, property taxes, medical expenses, and charitable contributions are among the most common itemized deductions. Maintain detailed records of qualified expenses to maximize your itemized deductions. Use tax software or a professional tax preparer to guarantee that you claim all applicable deductions. Consider "bunching" deductions, which is when you consolidate deductions into a single year to exceed the standard deduction limit.

Tax credits lower your tax bill dollar for dollar. Common tax breaks include the Child Tax Credit, Education Credits, and Energy Credits. Investigate available tax credits and ensure you meet the eligibility requirements. Claim all available tax credits to decrease your total tax liability. For example, if you are qualified for education credits, make sure to claim them to help cover the expense of continuing education.

Capital gains tax is a tax on the profits made from the sale of an asset. Long-term capital gains on assets held for more than a year are taxed at a lower rate than short-term gains. Plan your investing strategy to benefit from long-term capital gains rates. Tax-loss harvesting allows you to offset gains with losses and minimize your tax bill. For example, sell underperforming investments to offset profits from higher-performing ones.

Tax-deferred accounts allow you to defer paying taxes on contributions and earnings until withdrawal. Common tax-deferred accounts are 401(k)s, regular IRAs, and deferred compensation plans. Increase your contributions to these accounts to minimize your current tax-deductible income. Plan your withdrawals intelligently to help you manage your tax bracket in retirement. For example, to lessen the tax impact, make withdrawals during years with lower income.

Roth IRAs and Health Savings Accounts (HSAs) are tax-free accounts. Contributions to these accounts are made after taxes, but withdrawals are tax-free under certain conditions. Contribute to tax-free accounts to diversify your tax risk and benefit from tax-free growth. Plan your withdrawals from these accounts to best suit your overall tax strategy. Use an HSA to cover eligible medical expenses, and the savings will grow tax-free for future healthcare needs.

The Alternative Minimum Tax (AMT) is a parallel tax system designed to ensure that high-income people pay the bare minimum of taxes. Understand the AMT and how it can influence your tax liability. Plan your income and deductions to reduce your exposure to the AMT. Use tax software or visit a tax professional to see if you are liable for the AMT and plan accordingly.

Retirement contributions provide large tax savings. Contributions to a 401(k), IRA, or other retirement plan can lower your taxable income. Take advantage of employer-sponsored plans, especially those that provide matching contributions. Maximize your annual contributions to benefit from tax-deferred growth and potential tax deductions.

Health Savings Accounts (HSAs) offer three tax advantages: tax-deductible contributions, tax-free growth, and tax-free withdrawals for eligible medical costs. If your health plan has a high deductible, consider contributing to an HSA. HSA funds can be used for current medical bills or allowed to grow to cover future healthcare costs. Maximize donations to gain from tax breaks.

Flexible Spending Accounts (FSAs) enable you to save pre-tax cash for healthcare and dependent care expenses. Contribute to an FSA to lower your taxable income and pay for qualified costs with tax-free funds. Plan your contributions carefully, as FSAs are usually "use it or lose it" during the plan year.

If you itemize your deductions, charitable contributions may provide tax benefits. Donate cash or appreciated assets to a qualifying charitable organization. Keep track of your donations and get receipts for contributions above $250. Consider donating appreciated stocks to avoid paying capital gains taxes while still earning a charity deduction.

Education savings schemes, such as 529 plans, provide tax benefits for saving for educational expenses. Contributions grow tax-free, as do withdrawals for eligible educational costs. Use 529 plans to fund your children's or grandchildren's education. Consider making front-loading contributions to optimize tax benefits over time.

Tax-efficient investing entails ways to reduce taxes on your investments. Hold investments for at least a year to qualify for lower long-term capital gains rates. Use tax-advantaged accounts to hold tax-inefficient investments like bonds and real estate investment trusts. Invest in tax-efficient funds, such as index funds and ETFs, to minimize capital gains distributions.

Income shifting tactics entail transferring income from higher-taxed companies to lower-taxed ones. This can include hiring family members or transferring investments to family members with lower tax brackets. To avoid any complications, be familiar with IRS rules and regulations. Consult a tax specialist to successfully apply income-shifting solutions.

Estate planning is vital for effectively managing estate taxes and transferring wealth. Use trusts, gifting schemes, and other estate planning instruments to reduce estate taxes and ensure that your assets are transferred as you desire. Consult with an estate planning attorney to develop a comprehensive strategy that addresses both your tax and financial objectives.

Professional counsel is crucial when negotiating complex tax methods. Consider dealing with a CPA or tax expert who has experience working with physicians. Seek help with tax preparation, investment ideas, and retirement planning. Regularly check your tax situation with your advisor to ensure you are taking advantage of all possible tax breaks.

Research and education are critical for remaining current on tax tactics and legislation. Continue to educate yourself on tax laws, investing methods, and financial planning. Use reliable sources of knowledge, such as tax planning books, online courses, and financial journals. Stay informed on changes in tax rules and regulations so that you may alter your plans accordingly.

Tax techniques are essential for managing your finances and generating wealth. Physicians can establish a tax-efficient financial plan that enhances wealth while minimizing tax burden by knowing the fundamentals of taxation and taking action. Regularly assess and alter your tax tactics to stay on track and meet your long-term financial objectives.

Actionable Steps

☐ Contribute to tax-deferred accounts (401(k), IRA) to lower taxable income.

☐ Utilize tax-free accounts (Roth IRA, HSA) for tax-free growth and withdrawals.

☐ Implement tax-efficient investing strategies, such as holding investments for over a year for lower capital gains rates.

☐ Claim all available tax credits and deductions to reduce overall tax liability.

☐ Consult a tax professional to optimize tax planning and stay updated on tax laws and regulations.

Chapter 10

Insurance

"Fun is like life insurance; the older you get, the more it costs."

Kin Hubbard

Insurance is an important component of financial planning since it protects you, your family, and your assets against unforeseen circumstances. Understanding the various types of insurance and their value can assist physicians in providing comprehensive coverage. Begin by studying the fundamentals and practical procedures for selecting the appropriate insurance plans.

Insurance Coverage Types	
Health	Covers medical expenses
Life	Provides financial support to beneficiaries
Disability	Replaces income if you become disabled
Auto	Covers vehicle damage and liability
Homeowner's	Protects home and personal property

Life insurance provides financial security for your beneficiaries in the event of your death. It is critical for physicians to safeguard their families' financial stability. There are two forms of life insurance: term and whole life. Term life insurance provides coverage for a set length of time, whereas whole life insurance provides coverage for the rest of one's life, including cash value. Assess your family's financial needs and select a policy that provides enough coverage.

Term life insurance is an affordable way to offer coverage for a set length of time, such as 10, 20, or 30 years. Choose term life insurance if you only need coverage for a short period of time, such as until your children reach adulthood or your mortgage is paid off. Determine the appropriate coverage amount depending on your income, debts, and projected financial responsibilities. Compare quotes from different insurers to discover the best deal.

Whole life insurance provides everlasting coverage and has a cash value component that accumulates over time. If you want long-term protection as well as savings, go with whole life insurance. Be aware that whole life insurance costs more than term life insurance. Consult with an insurance professional to see if whole life insurance is right for you.

Disability insurance covers your income in case you are unable to work due to illness or injury. It is critical for physicians since their capacity to earn a living is their most significant asset. There are two forms of disability insurance: short-term and long-term. Short-term disability insurance offers coverage for a few months, but long-term disability insurance covers a longer period of time, maybe until retirement. Ensure that you have enough long-term disability insurance to replace a significant portion of your income.

Own-occupation disability insurance pays payments if you are unable to execute the obligations of your specific occupation. This is especially significant for physicians since it assures coverage even if they can work in another role but not in their specialty. Check that your policy includes own-occupation coverage for full protection.

Health insurance is vital for covering medical bills and avoiding exorbitant healthcare costs. Select a health insurance plan that provides appropriate coverage for your needs, such as preventive care, specialist visits, and prescription drugs. If you are employed, take advantage of company-sponsored health insurance programs. If you are self-employed, look into individual health insurance options or consider joining a professional association that provides group health insurance.

Long-term care insurance pays for long-term care services like nursing homes, home health care, and assisted living facilities. This form of insurance is critical for safeguarding your assets and ensuring you get the care you require in the future. If you are concerned about your future care needs, look into long-term care insurance and consider acquiring one. Compare policy details, pricing, and coverage alternatives.

Liability insurance protects you from financial losses if you are proven legally accountable for causing injury or damage to another person. This comprises both personal liability and professional liability insurance (malpractice insurance). Personal liability insurance is usually included in homeowner or renter insurance packages. To protect themselves from malpractice claims, physicians must carry professional liability insurance. Ensure that you have appropriate coverage to protect your personal and professional assets.

Professional liability insurance (malpractice insurance) is developed exclusively for doctors and other healthcare professionals. It protects you from claims of medical carelessness or malpractice. Ensure that your policy addresses the specific risks connected with your profession and practice setting. Regularly examine and update your coverage to reflect any changes in your practice.

Homeowners insurance covers damage or loss to your house and personal possessions caused by catastrophes such as fire, theft, or natural disasters. It also includes liability coverage in case someone is injured on your premises. Ensure that your policy adequately covers the value of your home and personal items. Consider adding coverage to high-value things like jewelry or art.

Renters insurance offers similar coverage to homeowners insurance, but it is intended for those who rent their houses. It protects your personal belongings and provides liability coverage. Make sure your policy covers the cost of replacing your things and includes liability coverage.

Auto insurance protects you from financial losses in the event of an automobile accident. It protects against property damage, medical expenditures, and liability for injuries or damages caused to others. Check that your policy provides appropriate coverage for liability, collision, and comprehensive damage. Consider providing supplemental coverage to uninsured or underinsured motorists.

Umbrella insurance extends liability coverage beyond the limits of your homeowner's, auto, and other basic insurance policies. It provides additional protection against big claims and lawsuits. If you have large assets to safeguard, you should consider obtaining umbrella insurance coverage. Determine the appropriate coverage quantity depending on your net worth and probable liability concerns.

If you own or operate a medical practice, you will need business insurance. It provides a variety of coverage options, including property insurance, liability insurance, and business interruption insurance. Ensure that your company's insurance coverage covers all of the hazards involved with your practice. Regularly examine and update your coverage to reflect changes in your company.

Business owners should get life and disability insurance to protect their businesses and maintain continuity. Key person insurance provides financial protection in the event that a key employee or partner gets disabled or dies. Business overhead expense insurance protects business expenses in the event that you become handicapped. Consult with an advisor about your business insurance needs to ensure you have comprehensive coverage.

Insurance policies should be reviewed on a regular basis to verify that your coverage is adequate and current. Review your policies once a year or if there are substantial life events, like marriage, childbirth, or purchasing a new house. Adjust your coverage to reflect changes in your financial status and risk exposure.

Consulting with insurance professionals can help you manage the complexity of insurance and ensure you have adequate coverage. Consult with insurance brokers or experts who specialize in dealing with physicians. Seek assistance on how to choose and manage insurance coverage to safeguard your financial interests.

Actionable Steps

☐ Ensure you have both term and whole life insurance to provide financial security for your family.

☐ Obtain disability insurance, especially own-occupation coverage, to protect your income in case of illness or injury.

☐ Select a comprehensive health insurance plan that covers preventive care, specialists, and prescriptions.

☐ Acquire liability insurance, including personal and professional (malpractice) coverage, to protect against legal claims.

☐ Regularly review and update your insurance policies to ensure adequate coverage and reflect any changes in your life circumstances.

Chapter 11

Risk Management

"The biggest risk is not taking any risk. In a world that is changing really quickly, the only strategy that is guaranteed to fail is not taking risks."

Mark Zuckerberg

Risk management is an important aspect of financial planning because it helps physicians protect their wealth and assets from potential risks. Understanding different risk management tactics can help you avoid financial losses and maintain long-term financial stability. Start by studying the foundations and practical strategies for effective risk management.

Identifying risks is the first step toward risk management. Income loss, malpractice lawsuits, investment volatility, and unexpected personal expenses are among the most common hazards faced by physicians. Conduct a thorough financial review to identify potential hazards. Consider the hazards linked to your profession, personal life, and investments. Use a risk assessment checklist to ensure you've covered all bases.

Income loss can occur as a result of disability, disease, or job loss. Protecting your income is critical to financial stability. Ensure that you have enough disability insurance to cover a major percentage of your income if you are unable to work. If the coverage provided by your work is insufficient, consider getting extra disability insurance. Create an emergency fund that will cover at least six months of living expenses.

Malpractice risk is a major worry for doctors. Professional liability insurance (malpractice insurance) provides coverage against claims of medical carelessness or malpractice. Ensure that your policy addresses the specific risks connected with your profession and practice setting. Regularly examine and update your coverage to reflect any changes in your practice. Implement risk management procedures in your firm to limit the chance of malpractice lawsuits.

Investment risk refers to the possibility of financial loss as a result of market volatility or poor investment performance. Diversifying your portfolio reduces investment risk. Diversify your investments among asset classes, including equities, bonds, real estate, and alternative investments. Review and rebalance your portfolio on a regular basis to ensure that your asset allocation and risk tolerance remain consistent.

Personal hazards include illnesses, accidents, and natural calamities. Health insurance, life insurance, and homeowners or renters insurance all help to mitigate these risks. Make sure you have appropriate coverage for medical expenditures, property damage, and liability. Consider getting supplementary coverage for high-value objects or specific risks, like flood or earthquake insurance. Regularly evaluate your insurance coverage to ensure it matches your requirements.

Emergency funds are an important aspect of risk management. An emergency fund serves as a financial buffer for unexpected expenses or income losses. Aim to save three to six months' worth of living costs in a liquid, easily accessible account. Make regular contributions to your emergency fund and adjust the amount as your financial circumstances change.

Debt management is critical to reducing financial risk. High debt levels can put a strain on your finances and make you more vulnerable to economic downturns and personal emergencies. Create a debt payback plan that prioritizes paying off high-interest debt first. Consider combining or refinancing debts to lower your interest rates and monthly payments. Avoid taking on more debt unless absolutely required and controllable.

Asset protection means protecting your assets against future creditors or legal demands. Asset protection strategies include titling assets in a way that gives legal protection, establishing trusts, and owning businesses through legal structures such as limited liability companies (LLCs). Consult an estate planning attorney to create an asset protection strategy that is consistent with your financial objectives and legal obligations.

Insurance reviews should be undertaken on a regular basis to ensure that your coverage is adequate and current. Review your insurance coverage every year or if there are substantial life events, such as marriage, childbirth, or purchasing a new house. Adjust your coverage to reflect changes in your financial status and risk exposure.

Estate planning is an important part of risk management because it guarantees that your assets are allocated according to your intentions while minimizing potential legal and tax complications for your descendants. Make a complete estate plan that includes a will, trusts, and powers of attorney. Designate beneficiaries for your retirement savings and keep them updated on a regular basis. Consult with an estate planning professional to ensure that your estate plan satisfies your objectives and legal requirements.

Tax planning helps to reduce the possibility of unexpected tax bills. Understand your tax requirements and use ways to reduce your tax load. Use tax-advantaged accounts, such as IRAs and 401(k)s, to lower taxable income while growing your savings tax-deferred. Consult a tax professional to create a tax strategy that is consistent with your financial objectives and risk tolerance.

Legal risk management means identifying and minimizing any legal concerns that may impact your finances. This includes ensuring regulatory compliance, preserving adequate documentation, and obtaining legal representation as needed. For physicians, this frequently entails remaining educated on changes in healthcare laws and regulations that affect their practice. Consider working with a healthcare attorney to ensure that your practice meets all legal standards.

Cybersecurity is becoming increasingly crucial in risk management, particularly among physicians who handle sensitive patient information. Implement strong cybersecurity procedures to prevent data breaches and cyberattacks. Use strong passwords, encryption, and secured networks. Train your employees on optimal data security procedures, and update your systems on a regular basis to address potential risks.

Professional counsel is crucial in navigating the complexity of risk management. Consider dealing with financial advisors, insurance brokers, estate planning attorneys, and tax professionals who have experience working with physicians. Seek assistance in creating and implementing a thorough risk management strategy. Regularly assess your risk management plans with your advisors to ensure they are in line with your financial objectives and the changing risk landscape.

Actionable Steps

☐ Conduct a thorough financial review to identify risks such as income loss, malpractice lawsuits, investment volatility, and unexpected personal expenses.

☐ Secure adequate coverage including disability, health, life, professional liability (malpractice), and homeowners or renters insurance to protect against various risks.

☐ Spread investments across different asset classes such as equities, bonds, real estate, and alternative investments to minimize risk.

☐ Save three to six months' worth of living expenses in a liquid, easily accessible account to cover unexpected expenses or income loss.

☐ Annually review and adjust insurance policies, estate plans, and financial strategies to ensure they align with your current needs and risks.

Chapter 12

Practice Financial Management

> *"In business, you don't get what you deserve, you get what you negotiate."*
>
> **Chester L. Karrass**

Physicians who own or operate a medical practice must manage their practice finances effectively. Effective financial management keeps the practice viable, sustainable, and able to provide high-quality care. Begin by studying the principles and processes for managing your medical practice's finances.

Revenue cycle management refers to the process of managing patient billing and payments. Efficient revenue cycle management is critical to ensuring cash flow and financial stability. Implement a strong billing system to ensure that claims are submitted accurately and on time. Monitor the revenue cycle on a frequent basis to detect and fix any difficulties as they arise. Train employees on the best billing and coding standards to reduce errors and claim denials.

Expense control is crucial for staying profitable. Regularly examine and analyze practice expenses to discover cost-cutting opportunities. Implement cost-cutting strategies such as negotiating with suppliers and maximizing resource utilization. Create a budget to track and regulate expenses, ensuring that spending is consistent with practice goals.

Cash flow management guarantees that the practice has enough funds to meet its operational costs. Create a cash flow statement to track the inflow and outflow of funds. Maintain a cash reserve to cover any unforeseen expenses or revenue deficits. Review cash flow estimates on a regular basis to anticipate and respond to prospective financial difficulties.

Financial statements represent a snapshot of the practice's financial health. The income statement, balance sheet, and cash flow statement are among the most important financial statements. Regularly evaluate these statements to determine the practice's profitability, liquidity, and financial situation. Use financial ratios and benchmarks to assess performance and pinpoint opportunities for improvement.

Budgeting is vital for planning and managing practice finances. Create an annual budget, including expected revenue and costs. Compare actual and budgeted financial performance on a regular basis to spot variances and alter plans accordingly. Include important employees in the budgeting process to guarantee buy-in and responsibility.

Accounts receivable management entails tracking and collecting payments due to this practice. Implement rules and procedures to ensure timely invoicing and follow-up on late bills. Use aging reports to keep track of outstanding receivables and prioritize collection activities. Consider giving payment options to patients to help them make regular payments.

Debt management is critical to sustaining financial stability. Monitor and manage practice debt, including loans for equipment, real estate, and working capital. Create a debt payback plan to ensure on-time payments and prevent default. Consider refinancing high-interest debt to lower interest rates and increase cash flow.

Tax planning helps to reduce the practice's tax liability and assure compliance with tax legislation. Consult with a tax professional to devise techniques for lowering taxable income, such as maximizing deductions and credits. Make anticipated tax payments to avoid penalties and interest. Maintain accurate records of all financial transactions to assist with tax filings.

Insurance is vital for safeguarding the practice from financial hazards. Ensure that the practice has enough coverage, which includes malpractice, general liability, property, and business interruption insurance. Regularly examine insurance plans to verify that they match the practice's needs and alter coverage as needed.

Compliance with healthcare rules is essential to avoid legal and financial fines. Stay up to date on changes in regulations that influence your practice, such as billing and coding rules, patient privacy laws, and employment regulations. Implement rules and procedures to ensure compliance, and perform frequent audits to detect and resolve any problems.

Financial benchmarking refers to comparing the practice's financial performance to industry standards. Use benchmarks to determine where the practice excels and where it needs to improve. Participate in industry surveys and read benchmarking studies to get useful information. Use this data to establish financial objectives and monitor progress.

Technology and automation can help to increase financial management efficiency. Invest in practice management software to automate billing, scheduling, and financial reporting. Use EHR systems to increase documentation and coding accuracy. Implement automation tools to reduce administrative workload and errors.

Strategic planning entails establishing long-term goals for the practice and devising strategies to attain them. Conduct a SWOT analysis (Strengths, Weaknesses, Opportunities, and Threats) to determine strategic priorities. Create a business plan that includes growth strategy, financial predictions, and important performance metrics. Regularly review and revise the plan to reflect market and practice changes.

Financial transparency with employees is critical for creating a culture of accountability and engagement. Share financial information with important staff members so they can better grasp the practice's financial goals and difficulties. Engage employees in financial decision-making processes to foster teamwork and ownership.

Patient volume management is critical for sustaining income and maximizing resource use. Monitor patient volume trends and put in place measures to attract and retain patients. Use marketing and outreach strategies to promote the practice and increase patient loyalty. Optimize scheduling to reduce wait times while increasing provider productivity.

A cost-benefit analysis can help you assess the financial implications of your practice decisions. Use a cost-benefit analysis to determine the prospective return on investment for new equipment, technology, or services. When making decisions, take into account both financial and non-financial rewards. Use this study to identify the investments that will provide the most value to the practice.

Financial advisors, accountants, and practice management experts can offer useful insights and support. Consider partnering with healthcare specialists to create and implement efficient financial management methods. Regularly examine the practice's financial performance with your advisors to ensure it is in line with your objectives.

Actionable Steps

☐ Develop a strong billing system, monitor revenue cycles, and train staff to reduce errors and claim denials.

☐ Regularly review expenses, negotiate with suppliers, and create a budget to track and control spending.

☐ Create and regularly review a cash flow statement, maintain a cash reserve, and anticipate potential financial challenges.

☐ Stay updated on healthcare regulations, implement compliance procedures, and secure comprehensive insurance coverage.

☐ Partner with financial advisors, invest in practice management software, and use automation tools to enhance financial management efficiency.

Chapter 13

Business Ownership

"A small business is an amazing way to serve and leave an impact on the world you live in."

Nicole Snow

Physicians can benefit from business ownership while also facing challenges. Owning a medical practice necessitates a mix of professional knowledge and business ability. Effective business management ensures that the practice runs smoothly, stays profitable, and provides excellent patient care. Start by studying the principles and practical steps to successful business ownership.

Choosing a business structure is an important first step. Common business formats include sole proprietorship, partnership, limited liability company (LLC), and corporation. Each structure carries unique legal, tax, and liability considerations. Consult a lawyer or a financial expert to identify the optimal structure for your practice. An LLC or company usually provides liability protection, which is essential for physicians.

Business plan development is critical for establishing goals and laying out a strategy to attain them. A thorough business plan consists of an executive summary, market analysis, organizational structure, services provided, marketing strategy, financial predictions, and funding requirements. Use your business plan as a road map for running and expanding your practice. Regularly review and update the plan to reflect changes in your company's environment.

Your practice may be funded through personal savings, bank loans, lines of credit, or investors. Determine your finance requirements based on startup expenditures, equipment purchases, and initial operational expenses. If you are looking for external money, prepare a clear financial plan and loan application. Investigate options such as SBA loans and medical practice financing programs.

Location selection is critical to recruiting patients and assuring the practice's success. Consider the following factors: visibility, accessibility, competition, and area demography. Conduct a thorough market analysis to determine the optimal location for your firm. Negotiate attractive leasing terms and make sure the facility fulfills your operational requirements.

A medical practice must be licensed and in compliance with regulations. Obtain all required licenses and permits, including as state medical licenses, DEA registration, and business licenses. Maintain compliance with healthcare requirements like HIPAA, OSHA, and CLIA. Create policies and procedures to ensure regulatory compliance and avoid legal difficulties.

Hiring talented experts to assist your clinical and administrative needs is part of the practice staffing process. Physicians, nurses, medical assistants, receptionists, billing specialists, and office managers are all key positions. Create clear job descriptions and hire candidates who have the necessary abilities and expertise for each position. Create a positive work atmosphere to recruit and retain top personnel.

Training and development are vital for keeping your employees competent and motivated. Provide continual training to help improve clinical skills, administrative efficiency, and patient care. Encourage professional development and provide incentives for Continuing Education. Regularly assess staff performance and provide constructive criticism.

Financial management is crucial to ensuring profitability and sustainability. Establish strong accounting systems to monitor sales, expenses, and cash flow. Create a budget and track financial performance against it. Assess the financial health of the practice using financial statements such as income and balance sheets. Work with a financial expert or accountant to improve your financial management.

Revenue cycle management refers to the process of managing patient billing and payments. Implement effective billing systems to ensure accurate and timely claim submission. Monitor the revenue cycle on a frequent basis to detect and fix any difficulties as they arise. Train employees on best billing and coding standards to reduce errors and claim denials.

Expense management contributes to cost control and profitability improvement. Regularly examine and analyze practice expenses to discover cost-cutting opportunities. Implement cost-cutting strategies such as negotiating with suppliers and maximizing resource utilization. Create a budget to track and regulate expenses, ensuring that spending is consistent with practice goals.

Marketing and patient acquisition are critical to growing your practice. Create a complete marketing strategy that combines online and offline techniques. Use digital marketing tools like a professional website, SEO, social media, and email marketing. Engage in community outreach and networking to foster ties and attract new patients.

Patient happiness and retention are crucial to the long-term success of your practice. Concentrate on providing high-quality care and a nice patient experience. Implement patient feedback systems, including as questionnaires, to get insight and suggest areas for improvement. Develop strong patient relationships through clear communication and individualized care.

Technology and automation can boost efficiency and patient care. Invest in practice management software to automate administrative activities like scheduling, billing, and financial reporting. Use electronic health record (EHR) technologies to improve documentation and patient care. Implement automation tools to reduce administrative workload and errors.

Risk management entails recognizing and addressing any threats to your practice. Ensure that you have enough insurance coverage, which includes malpractice, general liability, and property insurance. Implement rules and procedures to mitigate potential risks, including as data breaches, regulatory compliance difficulties, and worker safety. Regularly examine and update your risk management strategy.

Contracts, employment agreements, and labor-law compliance are all legal considerations. Collaborate with a healthcare attorney to create and analyze contracts with employees, suppliers, and service providers. Comply with employment rules such as pay and hour restrictions, anti-discrimination laws, and workplace safety standards. To avoid disagreements and potential liabilities, resolve legal matters as soon as possible.

Succession planning guarantees that your practice continues even if you retire, become disabled, or experience other unexpected situations. Create a succession plan outlining the steps for shifting ownership and management. Identify and develop prospective successors in your practice. Consider selling the practice, merging with another practice, or transferring ownership to a partner or family member.

Networking and professional development are essential for staying current and engaged in the healthcare business. Join professional associations, attend conferences, and pursue continuing education opportunities. Connect with other physicians and healthcare workers to exchange ideas, information, and support. Stay up to date on industry developments and best practices to help you enhance your practice.

Patient-centered care is the cornerstone of any successful medical practice. Focus on providing compassionate, high-quality treatment that is tailored to your patients' needs and preferences. Implement patient-centered practices like shared decision-making, tailored treatment plans, and clear communication. Continuously look for methods to improve the patient experience and health outcomes.

Actionable Steps

☐ Choose the right business structure (LLC, corporation).

☐ Develop a comprehensive business plan.

☐ Secure funding and select an optimal location.

☐ Hire and train competent staff.

☐ Implement effective financial and revenue cycle management.

Chapter 14

Estate Planning

"It's not about how much money you make, but how much money you keep, how hard it works for you, and how many generations you keep it for."

Robert Kiyosaki

Estate planning is critical for managing your assets, protecting your family's financial future, and ensuring that your intentions are followed out after you die. Effective estate planning combines legal documents, financial strategy, and tax preparation. Begin by understanding the fundamentals and practical methods for developing a thorough estate plan.

Wills are legal papers that define how your assets should be transferred upon your death. A will permits you to choose beneficiaries, appoint an executor to administer your inheritance, and assign guardians to minor children. Create a will that expresses your wishes clearly, and keep it up to date to reflect changes in your family or financial circumstances. Consult an estate planning professional to ensure that your will is legally legitimate and complete.

Trusts are legal arrangements in which a trustee manages assets on behalf of beneficiaries. Trusts can give tax advantages, shield assets from creditors, and facilitate asset transfers. Common trust kinds include revocable living trusts, irrevocable trusts, and special needs trusts. Consult with an estate planning expert to evaluate the best trust choices for your needs and to create the necessary legal documents.

A power of attorney (POA) gives someone the ability to make financial and legal decisions on your behalf if you become incapacitated. A durable power of attorney stays in effect if you are unable to make choices. Designate a trustworthy person as your POA and make sure they understand your intentions and responsibilities. Create a power of attorney document and have it notarized to make it legally binding.

If you are unable to make healthcare choices for yourself, you can designate someone to do so on your behalf. This individual should be aware of your medical preferences and willing to advocate for your wishes. Create a healthcare proxy paperwork and share your healthcare preferences with your appointed proxy.

Living wills, also known as advance directives, state your desires for medical treatment in the event that you become incapacitated and unable to convey your decisions. These documents may include preferences for life-sustaining treatment, resuscitation, or organ donation. Create a living will that clearly states your medical wishes and distribute it to your healthcare proxy and medical professionals.

Beneficiary designations are critical for assets such as retirement plans, life insurance policies, and payable-on-death (POD) accounts. Make sure your beneficiary designations are up to date and match your current intentions. Beneficiary designations should be reviewed and updated on a regular basis, particularly following major life events such as marriage, divorce, or childbirth.

Estate taxes have a substantial impact on the value of your estate. Understanding federal and state estate tax regulations might help you devise tax-saving measures. Use estate planning instruments like trusts, gifting techniques, and charity donations to decrease your estate's taxable worth. Collaborate with a tax professional to create successful tax planning methods.

Gifting involves transferring assets to beneficiaries during your lifetime in order to lower the amount of your taxable estate. The annual gift tax exclusion allows you to give a specific amount to each recipient while avoiding gift taxes. Consider giving regular donations to family members or creating a trust to administer the money. Consult an estate planning attorney to learn about the tax implications and benefits of gifting.

Donations to charitable organizations can provide tax breaks while also supporting causes close to your heart. Consider making philanthropic bequests in your will or establishing a charity trust. Donations to approved charities can help you save money on your inheritance taxes while also leaving a lasting legacy. Work with a financial advisor to create a charity giving strategy that reflects your values and financial objectives.

Digital estate planning entails managing your digital assets, which include internet accounts, social media profiles, and digital files. Create an inventory of your digital assets and include instructions for accessing and managing them. Designate a digital executor to manage your digital estate and ensure that your intentions are fulfilled. Incorporate digital estate planning into your overall estate plan to safeguard your online presence and digital legacy.

If you own a medical practice or any other type of business, you must plan for succession. Create a succession plan outlining the steps for shifting ownership and management. Identify and develop prospective successors in your practice. Consider selling the practice, merging with another practice, or transferring ownership to a partner or family member. Work with your legal and financial professionals to facilitate a smooth transition.

Life insurance can be quite beneficial in estate planning because it provides liquidity to cover estate taxes, debts, and other expenses. Your beneficiaries may potentially benefit financially from the earnings of your life insurance policy. Check your life insurance coverage to make sure it fits your estate planning requirements. Consider creating an irrevocable life insurance trust (ILIT) to keep policy proceeds out of your taxable estate.

Special needs planning entails making arrangements for a family member with special needs. Create a special needs trust to meet their financial needs while maintaining their eligibility for government assistance.

Work with an estate planning attorney to create a thorough plan that meets your family member's specific needs.

The executor's tasks include administering and distributing your estate according to your instructions. Choose an executor who is trustworthy, organized, and capable of carrying out the duties. Allow your executor access to essential documents and asset information. Discuss your preferences and expectations with your chosen executor to ensure they are ready for the task.

A periodic review of your estate plan is required to guarantee that it remains current and effective. Review your estate plan every a year or after a big life event, such as marriage, divorce, childbirth, or significant financial changes. Update your paperwork and beneficiary designations as necessary to reflect your current preferences and circumstances.

Actionable Steps

☐ Create and regularly update a will.

☐ Establish trusts for asset management.

☐ Designate power of attorney and healthcare proxy.

☐ Keep beneficiary designations current.

☐ Plan for estate taxes and gifting.

Chapter 15

Major Life Events

"The only thing constant in life is change."

Heraclitus

Navigating big life events entails knowing their financial ramifications and taking proactive measures to manage your money during these times. Marriage, divorce, having children, buying a property, and retiring can all have a substantial impact on your finances. Begin by studying the fundamentals and practical techniques for handling your funds throughout these occurrences.

Marriage combines two financial lives, thus it is critical to discuss and coordinate your financial objectives and plans with your partner. Begin by preparing a combined budget that includes both income and expenses. Decide whether to entirely consolidate finances, keep separate accounts, or do a hybrid of the two. Discuss financial goals such as home ownership, retirement, and future children's schooling. If one or both partners have substantial assets or obligations, think about drafting a prenuptial agreement.

Combining finances entails deciding between joint and separate accounts, bill payments, and savings plans.

Create joint accounts for shared expenses like mortgages, utilities, and food, but keep individual accounts for personal spending. Set up automated payments to joint savings and investment accounts to meet common financial goals. Regularly communicate about financial decisions and go over your budget together.

Divorce can have a huge financial impact, necessitating careful planning and management. Consult with a divorce attorney and a financial expert to better understand the financial implications of your divorce settlement. Determine and value marital assets, such as real estate, investments, retirement accounts, and personal property. Create a plan for distributing assets and debts fairly. Update your estate planning documents, such as wills, trusts, and beneficiary designations, to reflect your new status.

Childbirth and raising children need new financial duties and considerations. Begin by preparing a budget that covers expenses for childcare, healthcare, education, and daily necessities. Set up a savings account or a 529 plan to fund your child's education. Check and update your health insurance to ensure that it includes pregnancy and pediatric care. Consider obtaining life insurance to ensure financial security for your family in the event of your untimely death.

Adoption incurs additional costs, such as legal fees, travel expenses, and adoption agency fees. Look into available resources, such as workplace adoption perks, tax credits, and grants. Make a budget to cover these expenses and alter your financial goals accordingly. Consider working with an adoption financial advisor to help you negotiate the financial aspects of the adoption process.

Purchasing a home is a substantial financial investment that necessitates careful planning. Begin by evaluating your current financial condition, including your credit score, income, and savings. Determine how much you can afford to spend on a home, taking into account both the initial purchase price and continuing expenses such as property taxes, insurance, and maintenance. To avoid private mortgage insurance (PMI), save for a down payment of approximately 20% of the home's buying price. Consult a mortgage broker to determine the best loan terms and interest rates.

Selling a home entails preparing your property for sale, researching market circumstances, and collaborating with real estate agents. Begin by making the necessary repairs and renovations to raise your home's worth. To determine a competitive asking price, conduct research on comparable house sales in your area. Consider arranging your home to attract interested buyers. Work with a real estate agent to market your property and negotiate offers. Prepare for closing costs and taxes involved with the transaction.

Retirement necessitates careful financial preparation to ensure that you have enough money to maintain your preferred lifestyle. Begin by calculating your retirement expenses, which include housing, healthcare, travel, and leisure activities. Determine your retirement income options, including Social Security, pensions, retirement funds, and investments. Create a savings and investing strategy to meet your retirement objectives.

Consider working with a financial expert to develop a complete retirement strategy.

Caring for aging parents can have serious financial and emotional consequences. Begin by talking about your parents' financial condition, including their income, assets, debts, and expenses. Review their legal documents, such as wills, powers of attorney, and healthcare proxies, to ensure they are current. Consider long-term care choices such as home care, assisted living, and nursing facilities. Consider getting long-term care insurance to assist cover these expenses. Create a plan for sharing caregiving responsibilities with other family members.

Loss of a loved one is an emotionally difficult occurrence that also has financial consequences. Begin by notifying the appropriate organizations, such as banks, insurance companies, and government authorities, of the death. Obtain several copies of the death certificate for legal and financial reasons. Review and settle the deceased's estate, including debt payments and asset distribution in accordance with the will or state legislation. If necessary, see an estate attorney to guide you through the probate process. Consider receiving bereavement therapy to help with your emotional well-being.

To manage your spending and preserve stability following an unexpected job loss, you must immediately arrange your finances. Begin by applying for unemployment benefits to offer temporary income. Create a budget to prioritize critical expenses and find areas where you may save money. To keep your health insurance coverage, look at options like COBRA or marketplace plans. Update your résumé and start networking to uncover new career prospects. Consider using emergency funds or taking on temporary job to bolster your income.

Major health conditions can have a huge financial impact, necessitating cautious preparation and control. Examine your health insurance coverage to ensure that it fits your requirements, including out-of-pocket expenses and coverage for important procedures. Create a budget to cover medical expenses such as copays, prescriptions, and specialist appointments. Consider financial aid options such as charity care programs, patient assistance programs, and medical billing advocacy. Consider working with a financial expert to create a strategy for managing healthcare costs.

Financial windfalls, such as an inheritance, lottery winnings, or a large bonus, must be carefully managed to reap long-term rewards. Begin by meeting with a financial counselor to create a strategy for your windfall. Pay off high-interest debt and start an emergency fund if you don't already have one. Consider investing some of the windfall to increase your wealth over time. Be aware of the tax implications and set aside money to cover any tax liabilities. Avoid impulsive or excessive purchases.

Actionable Steps

☐ Coordinate finances and goals with your partner in marriage.

☐ Budget for childcare, healthcare, and education expenses when having children.

☐ Save for a down payment and consult a mortgage broker when buying a home.

☐ Calculate retirement expenses and create a savings and investing strategy.

☐ Apply for unemployment benefits and create a budget during job loss.

Chapter 16

Career Transitions

"Success is not the key to happiness. Happiness is the key to success. If you love what you are doing, you will be successful."

Albert Schweitzer

Career transitions can have a substantial influence on your finances, necessitating careful planning and management. Whether you are changing specialties, starting your own practice, pursuing academic opportunities, or retiring, understanding the financial consequences and taking preemptive actions will help you make a smooth transition. Begin by studying the fundamentals and practical strategies to manage your funds throughout a career transfer.

Changing specialty frequently necessitates further training, certification, or education, which might affect your earnings and expenses. Begin by investigating the requirements and fees involved with the new specialty. Create a budget to cover tuition, test fees, and any potential income loss during the transition period. Consider applying for scholarships, grants, or educational loans to assist fund your training. Prepare for a temporary loss in income and alter your lifestyle and financial goals accordingly.

Establishing your own practice necessitates extensive financial planning and investment. Begin by developing a detailed business plan that includes your objectives, target market, services provided, and financial projections. Determine your initial expenditures, which may include leasing or acquiring office space, purchasing medical equipment, employing employees, and obtaining relevant licenses and permissions. Secure funds via personal savings, bank loans, or investors. Create a budget to control ongoing spending, and keep track of your cash flow on a regular basis.

Joining a group practice or partnership entails knowing the financial and legal ramifications. Examine the provisions of the partnership agreement, such as profit-sharing, buy-in costs, and decision-making procedures. Evaluate the financial health and stability of the group practice. Consider working with a financial advisor and an attorney to analyze the partnership agreement and verify it is in line with your financial objectives and interests. Prepare for anticipated income fluctuations and make necessary budget adjustments.

Pursuing academic options like as teaching, research, or administration can have an impact on your salary and career. Consider the financial ramifications of moving to an academic position, such as prospective changes in income, benefits, and work-life balance. Think about the long-term career rewards, such as work security, professional development, and prospects for growth. Create a budget to manage income fluctuations and adapt your financial goals as needed.

Transitioning to non-clinical professions such as healthcare administration, consulting, or policymaking necessitates new skills and may impact your compensation. Determine the credentials and experience required for the new position, as well as the potential financial impact. Consider getting further schooling or certificates to improve your qualifications. Network with people in the field to obtain insights and find job possibilities. Create a budget to manage anticipated income fluctuations and alter your financial objectives accordingly.

Taking a sabbatical or extended leave for personal or professional reasons necessitates meticulous financial planning. Evaluate your financial condition and develop a budget to cover your expenses during the leave period. Ensure that you have enough savings to maintain yourself and your family. Consider how to preserve health insurance coverage and other benefits throughout your leave. Stay connected with professional networks and continue your education to ensure a smooth transition back into the workforce.

Understanding the financial ramifications of moving to a new region is essential when relocating for work. Investigate the cost of living, housing market, and job market in the new location. Create a budget to cover moving costs, such as transportation, interim accommodation, and relocation assistance. Negotiate relocation help with your new employment, if possible. Prepare for anticipated income fluctuations and make necessary budget adjustments.

Preparing for retirement is creating a complete financial plan to guarantee you have enough money to live your preferred lifestyle. Begin by calculating your retirement expenses, which include housing, healthcare, travel, and leisure activities. Determine your retirement income options, including Social Security, pensions, retirement funds, and investments. Create a savings and investing strategy to meet your retirement objectives. Consider working with a financial expert to develop a comprehensive retirement strategy.

Phased retirement is a way to gradually reduce your work hours while transitioning to complete retirement. Examine the financial ramifications of a phased retirement, including changes in income, benefits, and work-life balance. Create a budget to control your costs during the transition phase. Discuss phased retirement possibilities with your company and work out a strategy that suits your circumstances.

Mentoring and succession planning are critical for guaranteeing the longevity of your firm or professional legacy. Identify and mentor possible successors in your profession or organization. Create a succession plan outlining the steps for transitioning leadership and responsibilities. Consult with legal and financial professionals to facilitate a smooth transition and safeguard your interests.

Volunteering and part-time work can bring both fulfillment and supplementary cash in retirement. Investigate opportunities for volunteering or part-time job in areas that interest you. Think about the financial and personal rewards of remaining active and engaged in your community. Create a budget that includes any additional income and adjusts your financial goals as needed.

Building a professional network is critical for handling career changes successfully. Join professional associations, attend conferences, and pursue continuing education opportunities. Connect with other physicians and healthcare workers to exchange ideas, information, and support. To ensure a seamless transition, stay up to date on industry trends and career prospects.

Actionable Steps

☐ Research and budget for changing specialties if planning that route

☐ Develop a business plan for starting your own practice.

☐ Analyze financial and legal implications of joining a group practice.

☐ Evaluate financial impact of pursuing academic opportunities.

☐ Plan for retirement.

Chapter 17

Financial Education

"An investment in knowledge pays the best interest."

Benjamin Franklin

Ongoing financial education is essential for physicians to maintain and improve their financial literacy, adapt to changing financial environments, and make sound decisions. Continuous learning keeps you informed about new financial products, investing methods, tax rules, and economic developments. Begin by recognizing the value of continual financial education and how to incorporate it into your daily routine.

Staying current with financial news is critical for making informed judgments. Read financial publications and periodicals on a regular basis, as well as reliable internet sites like The Wall Street Journal, Bloomberg, and Financial Times. Subscribe to financial publications that cover market trends, investment techniques, and economic happenings. Set aside time each day or week to analyze financial news and keep up with the newest trends and changes.

Attending financial seminars and webinars allows you to learn from experts and obtain fresh ideas. Look for seminars and webinars offered by financial institutions, professional associations, and educational organizations. Participate in events covering subjects pertinent to physicians, such as retirement planning, tax strategies, and investment options. Take notes and ask questions to help you learn and apply new information to your financial planning.

Taking finance classes might help you gain in-depth knowledge and abilities. Enroll in classes through universities, community institutions, or online platforms such as Coursera, Udemy, and Khan Academy. Search for courses in personal finance, investing, real estate, retirement planning, and tax methods. Consider earning qualifications like Certified Financial Planner (CFP) or Chartered Financial Analyst (CFA) to expand your knowledge.

Reading financial books might help you broaden your knowledge and gain new insights. Make a reading list featuring well respected financial works by authors such as Benjamin Graham, Warren Buffett, Robert Kiyosaki, and Burton Malkiel. Begin with basic literature such as "The Intelligent Investor," "Rich Dad Poor Dad," and "A Random Walk Down Wall Street." Set aside regular time to read and consider how the lessons apply to your financial circumstances.

Joining professional associations grants you access to resources, networking opportunities, and educational activities. Consider joining organizations like the American Medical Association (AMA), the Financial Planning Association (FPA), or your local medical society. Attend conferences, workshops, and study groups to network with peers and remain current on industry trends. Make use of internet forums and discussion groups to share expertise and experience.

Working with a financial advisor provides personalized advice and knowledge. Select a financial advisor that specializes in working with physicians and understands your specific financial needs. Schedule regular meetings to go over your financial strategy, address any changes in your goals or circumstances, and adapt methods as necessary. Ask your advisor to offer educational materials and explain complicated financial topics.

Networking with peers can provide useful information and support. Join or create a financial study group with other physicians to discuss financial issues, share experiences, and learn from one another. Attend networking events, both in person and online, to meet other professionals interested in financial education. Use social media tools such as LinkedIn to join organizations and follow financial sector influencers.

Using financial planning tools and applications can help you manage your money more successfully and stay informed. Look at budgeting programs (such as Mint and YNAB), investment monitoring services (such as Personal Capital), and retirement planning calculators. Use these tools to track your financial progress, create goals, and make informed decisions. Review your financial data on a regular basis and make adjustments based on what you learn.

Reflecting on previous financial decisions allows you to learn from your experiences. Periodically analyze your financial decisions, both successful and unsuccessful, to uncover patterns and places for improvement. Consider keeping a financial journal to track your actions, justifications, and results. Use this reflection to improve your financial tactics and avoid repeating previous mistakes.

Adapting to changes in the financial landscape is critical to long-term success. Keep track of changes in tax laws, market conditions, and economic policies that may affect your financial plan. Be adaptable and open to alter your strategies in response to new opportunities and obstacles. Consult with your financial advisor to verify that your strategy remains in line with your objectives and current circumstances.

Self-assessment allows you to identify knowledge gaps and areas for improvement. Take online financial literacy quizzes and examinations to see how well you comprehend essential concepts. Set specific learning goals based on the data, and prioritize areas for improvement. To keep motivated, track your progress and celebrate milestones along the way.

Incorporating financial education into your everyday routine helps you stay informed and increase your financial literacy over time. Set aside time each day or week to read articles, watch videos, or listen to podcasts about financial matters. Make learning a habit by incorporating it into your everyday routine, such as reading financial news with your morning coffee or listening to podcasts on the commute.

Seeking feedback from reputable sources might help you gain fresh insights and enhance your financial tactics. Discuss your financial intentions and decisions with a financial counselor, mentor, or competent colleague. Be open to constructive criticism, and utilize it to improve your approach. Seek advice on your financial objectives, investing decisions, and risk management methods on a regular basis.

Actionable Steps

☐ Attend financial seminars and webinars to learn from experts and gain new insights.

☐ Take finance courses online or in person to deepen your knowledge.

☐ Read financial books to broaden your understanding.

☐ Work with financial advisors or educators who specializes in physicians' financial needs.

☐ Stay current with major financial news by reading publications and reliable online sources.

Chapter 18

Financial Plans

"A goal without a plan is just a wish."

Antoine de Saint-Exupéry

Reviewing and revising your financial plan is critical to ensuring that it remains in line with your objectives, circumstances, and market conditions. Regular evaluations and adjustments help you stay on track to meet your financial goals while also adapting to changes in your life and the overall economic situation. Begin by understanding the significance of regular financial evaluations and the practical procedures for properly revising your strategy.

Setting a review schedule guarantees that you regularly analyze your financial plan. Conduct a full assessment at least once a year, with extra reviews scheduled after important life events such as marriage, divorce, childbirth, or career change. Quarterly or semi-annual reviews might help you remain on top of your finances and make any modifications. Keep track of your review schedule with calendar reminders or financial planning software.

Assessing your financial goals entails comparing your short-term and long-term goals. Check your goals to make sure they are still relevant and attainable. Consider changes in your personal and professional life that may affect your goals, such as career progression, family planning, or health difficulties. Update your goals as needed and prioritize them according to their significance and timetable. Write out your revised goals and develop an action plan to attain them.

Evaluating your budget is critical for controlling your income and spending. Examine your budget to see where you may minimize expenses or reallocate funds. Compare your actual expenditure to your budgeted amounts, and revise your budget to reflect changes in your financial circumstances. Look for ways to raise your savings, minimize your debt, and improve your spending habits. Use budgeting tools or applications to keep track of your expenses and finances.

Monitoring your investments ensures they are consistent with your risk tolerance and financial objectives. Examine your financial portfolio to determine its performance and diversification. Check to see if your asset allocation is still appropriate for your risk tolerance and time horizon. Rebalance your portfolio as needed to keep your desired asset allocation. Consider working with a financial expert to assess your investing plan and make sound selections.

Reviewing your retirement plan keeps you on pace to achieve your retirement goals. Assess your retirement funds and compare them to your expected retirement needs. Consider inflation, healthcare expenditures, and life expectancy while analyzing your retirement plan. Increase your retirement contributions if necessary, and look into other retirement savings choices like IRAs or employer-sponsored plans. Refine your strategy with retirement planning tools or by consulting with a financial professional.

Reevaluating your insurance coverage protects your financial security. Examine your insurance policies, which include life, health, disability, and property insurance, to ensure that they provide appropriate coverage. Update your insurance to reflect life changes like marriage, childbirth, or buying a new house. Consider additional coverage if necessary, and shop around for better rates or terms. Consult an insurance advisor to evaluate your insurance needs and make informed selections.

Managing your debt entails frequently assessing your debt repayment strategy. Determine your present debt levels, interest rates, and repayment conditions. To save money on interest, pay off high-interest debt first and then consider consolidating or refinancing debts. Create a plan to pay off debt and avoid incurring new debt unless absolutely required. Use debt management tools or get advice from a financial counselor to develop a debt repayment strategy that works for you.

Evaluate your tax approach to reduce your tax liability and maximize your savings. Examine your tax situation for potential deductions, credits, and other tax-saving alternatives. Consider changes to tax laws and regulations that may affect your financial plan. Collaborate with a tax expert to create a complete tax strategy that is consistent with your financial objectives. Keep accurate records of your financial transactions to support your tax returns.

Updating your estate plan guarantees that your assets are dispersed in accordance with your preferences while minimizing potential legal and tax complications for your heirs. Check your will, trusts, power of attorney, and healthcare directives to make sure they represent your current preferences. Update your beneficiary designations for retirement accounts, life insurance plans, and other financial assets. Consult with an estate planning professional to make any required revisions and confirm that your estate plan is legally legitimate and complete.

Assessing your emergency fund is critical to financial stability. Examine the amount you've saved in your emergency fund to make sure it covers at least three to six months of living expenses. If your financial condition or risk exposure changes, consider expanding your emergency fund. Keep your emergency fund in a liquid, easily accessible account to guarantee that it is there when needed.

Major life events must be taken into account while developing a financial strategy. Identify any anticipated important life events, such as marriage, childbirth, home ownership, or retirement, and evaluate their possible influence on your finances. Update your financial plan to reflect these events, and build a budget to cover the corresponding costs. Collaborate with a financial advisor to create methods for handling these transitions successfully.

Financial planning software and applications can help you stay organized and informed. Look at budgeting programs (such as Mint and YNAB), investment monitoring services (such as Personal Capital), and retirement planning calculators. Use these tools to track your financial progress, create goals, and make informed decisions. Review your financial data on a regular basis and make adjustments based on what you learn.

Seeking expert assistance can help you manage your finances more effectively. Consider hiring a financial counselor, accountant, or estate planning attorney who specializes in working with physicians. Schedule regular meetings to go over your financial strategy, address any changes in your goals or circumstances, and adapt methods as necessary. Ask your advisor to offer educational materials and explain complicated financial topics.

Reflecting on previous financial decisions allows you to learn from them and improve your financial tactics. Periodically analyze your financial decisions, both successful and unsuccessful, to uncover patterns and places for improvement. Consider keeping a financial journal to track your actions, justifications, and results. Use this reflection to improve your financial tactics and avoid repeating previous mistakes.

Adapting to changes in the financial landscape is critical to long-term success. Keep track of changes in tax laws, market conditions, and economic policies that may affect your financial plan. Be adaptable and open to alter your strategies in response to new opportunities and obstacles. Consult with your financial advisor to verify that your strategy remains in line with your objectives and current circumstances.

Setting new financial goals keeps your plan fresh and relevant. Examine your progress toward current goals and set new ones as necessary. Consider both short-term goals, such as saving for a vacation or paying off a credit card, and long-term ones, such as buying a house or planning for retirement. Break down your goals into actual tasks and create a timeline for completing them.

Actionable Steps

☐ Conduct annual reviews of your financial plan and additional reviews after major life events.

☐ Regularly assess and adjust your short-term and long-term financial goals.

☐ Periodically review and adjust your investment portfolio to match your risk tolerance and objectives.

☐ Ensure your insurance coverage is adequate and update it as needed.

☐ Check and revise your will, trusts, and beneficiary designations to reflect current wishes.

www.ingramcontent.com/pod-product-compliance
Lightning Source LLC
Chambersburg PA
CBHW071833210526
45479CB00001B/121